MORMON HANDBOOK

Mormon Handbook

By Robert Holden

Copyright 2010-2011 General Management LLC

ISBN 978-1-257-95904-4

INTRODUCTION 8

METHODOLOGY 9
TERMS OF USE 9
SOURCES 10

TIMELINE OF KEY HISTORICAL EVENTS 12

FIRST VISION 14

CONTRADICTORY VERSIONS 16
FULL TEXTS 19

FIRST VISION PLAGIARIZED 24

FULL TEXTS 28

APOSTASY 35

CONDEMNING CHRISTIANITY 36
CONDEMNING THE CATHOLIC CHURCH 37
DISTRUST OF THE BIBLE 37
THE BOOK OF MORMON SPARED THE APOSTASY 39

SUCCESSION CRISIS 41

GENERAL AUTHORITIES 43

THE CANON 45

BOOK OF MORMON 45

BOOK OF MORMON ORIGINS 46
GOLD PLATES 48
BOOK OF MORMON WITNESSES 51
BOOK OF MORMON TRANSLATION 53

URIM AND THUMMIM	54
LOST 116 PAGES	**56**
ARCHAEOLOGY	**59**
NEW WORLD ARCHAEOLOGICAL FUNDING (NWAF)	61
SMITHSONIAN INSTITUTE	61
NATIONAL GEOGRAPHIC	61
BOOK OF MORMON LOCATIONS	**62**
BOUNTIFUL	64
HILL CUMORAH	67
NAHOM	72
BOOK OF MORMON AUTHORSHIP	**81**
5,000 CHANGES TO THE BOOK OF MORMON	**84**
DOCTRINAL CHANGES	84
CORRECTING ERRORS	87
FROM AUTHOR TO TRANSLATOR	88
ABSURDITIES IN THE BOOK OF MORMON	**91**
KING JAMES ENGLISH IN THE BOOK OF MORMON	**96**
WORDINESS	**98**
ANACHRONISMS	**100**
ANIMALS	100
AGRICULTURE	101
INDUSTRY	101
LINGUISTICS	102
THEOLOGY	104
PLAGIARIZING THE KING JAMES BIBLE	105
VIEW OF THE HEBREWS	**107**
ISAIAH IN THE BOOK OF MORMON	**112**
SHOULD I PRAY ABOUT THE BOOK OF MORMON?	**116**
THE BIBLICAL CRITERIA: FAITH + FACTS	117

DOCTRINE AND COVENANTS 118

LECTURES ON FAITH	120
DOCTRINE AND COVENANTS SECTION 2	124
DOCTRINE AND COVENANTS SECTION 5	125
DOCTRINE AND COVENANTS SECTION 13	126
DOCTRINE AND COVENANTS SECTION 20	127
DOCTRINE AND COVENANTS SECTION 27	128
DOCTRINE AND COVENANTS SECTION 48	130
DOCTRINE AND COVENANTS SECTION 101	131

PEARL OF GREAT PRICE 133

BOOK OF ABRAHAM 134
BOOK OF ABRAHAM FACSIMILE 1 141
BOOK OF ABRAHAM FACSIMILE 2 144
BOOK OF ABRAHAM FACSIMILE 3 147
BOOK OF ABRAHAM - KIRTLAND EGYPTIAN PAPERS 150

KING JAMES VERSION BIBLE 155

INSPIRED VERSION 155

JOURNAL OF DISCOURSES 156

OTHER SCRIPTURES 157

DEFINING MORMON DOCTRINE 158

THE GODHEAD 159

GOD IS AN EXALTED MAN 161
GOD IS ETERNALLY PROGRESSING 162
GOD HAS A BODY 165
POLYTHEISM 169
THE TRINITY IS COMPRISED OF THREE GODS 169
GOD THE FATHER HAS A FATHER 169
GOD THE FATHER IS MARRIED TO HEAVENLY MOTHER(S) 170
OTHER GODS 170
EXALTATION—MORMONS MAY BECOME GODS 181
KOLOB 182

ADAM GOD DOCTRINE 184

POLYGAMY 190

DOCTRINAL TEACHINGS ON POLYGAMY 201

PRIESTHOOD 204

RACISM 211

SALVATION 223

PRE-EARTH LIFE	223
LUCIFER	224
ATONEMENT AT GETHSEMANE	224
THREE HEAVENS: THREE DEGREES OF GLORY	225
SAVED BY WORKS	227
SALVATION THROUGH JOSEPH SMITH	227
CHRISTIANITY—SALVATION IN CHRIST ALONE	228
SALVATION BY FAITH NOT WORKS	229
ATONEMENT ON THE CROSS	230
MAN CREATED—NOT CONCEIVED	231
JESUS CREATED SATAN (LUCIFER)	232
THE BIBLICAL THREE HEAVENS	233
NEW HEAVEN AND NEW EARTH	235

TEMPLES 237

BAPTISMS FOR THE DEAD	239

THE MORMON TESTIMONY 242

JOSEPH SMITH 244

JOSEPH SMITH—MONEY DIGGER	245
JOSEPH SMITH—PROPHET	249
TESTING PROPHETS	254
JOSEPH SMITH—TRANSLATOR	256
KINDERHOOK PLATES	257

BRIGHAM YOUNG 262

THE MOON AND SUN INHABITED	263

B. H. ROBERTS 264

DAVID WHITMER 267

CHARLES ANTHON 272

MARK HOFFMAN 275

THOMAS FERGUSON **276**

CONTACT **278**

Introduction

The Mormon Handbook is a reference to *The Church of Jesus Christ of Latter-day Saints* (LDS), headquartered in Salt Lake City, Utah. It is not to be confused with the LDS *Church Handbook of Instructions*.

After the death of Joseph Smith, the church he founded split into several organizations. Those who sided with Brigham Young followed him to the Salt Lake basin, where today the LDS church is the largest of those who still regard Joseph a true prophet.

Members are called "Latter-day Saints" (LDS) or "Mormons", after the Book of Mormon, which purports to be "another testament of Jesus Christ". *LDS* and *Mormon* are used interchangeably throughout the handbook.

The Mormon church claims to be the only true Christian church today. Mormons believe that the original church founded by Jesus Christ went into apostasy soon after his apostles died, and was restored in 1830 by their prophet Joseph Smith. Mormons believe that the Bible and true doctrine were corrupted during this span, and believe that today's LDS church is nearly identical to the original church.

Because the Mormon church claims to be the only true Christian church, the handbook presents a comparison between Mormonism and Christianity.

Methodology

Because Mormonism is a complex and controversial religion, the goal of the handbook is to present facts in a concise, bullet-point format.

- Topics that are trivial or lack adequate documentation are avoided.
- Most references and quotes are from church friendly sources and church leaders.
- Reputable professionals are quoted in their respective field of study.
- Every effort has been made to ensure that quotes are used in context.
- Biblical quotes are from the *King James Version* unless noted otherwise.

Terms of Use

All Rights Reserved.

Articles within may be freely distributed provided the work is fully credited and is not used for any pecuniary purposes. Entire articles may not be reproduced in any electronic format accessible to the internet.

Sources

A list of key sources referenced and quoted in the handbook.

Dates	Publication
1611	**The Holy Bible** King James Version
1815	**The Religious Experience of Norris Stearns** By Norris Stearns. Considered source material for Joseph Smith's *First Vision*.
1816	**The Life, Conversion, Preaching, Travel, and Sufferings of Elias Smith** By Elias Smith. Considered source material for Joseph Smith's *First Vision*. **A Short Sketch of the Life of Solomon Chamberlain** By Solomon Chamberlain. Considered source material for Joseph Smith's *First Vision*.
1821	**Memoirs of Revival of Religion** By Charles Finney. Considered source material for Joseph Smith's *First Vision*.
1823, 1825	**View of the Hebrews** By Ethan Smith. About ancient Jews migrating to the Americas. Considered source material for Joseph Smith's *Book of Mormon*. Second edition published in 1825.
1830	**Book of Mormon, Original Edition**
1830-1833	**Inspired Version** Joseph Smith's translation of the (KJV) Bible.
1832	**History of the Life of Joseph Smith** By Joseph Smith
1832-1834	**Evening and Morning Star** Official church periodical. Replaced by *Messenger and Advocate*.
1833	**Doctrine and Covenants, Original Edition** The original edition was named *Book of Commandments*. The second edition was published in 1835 and renamed *Doctrine and Covenants*.
1834-1837	**Messenger and Advocate** Official church periodical. Replaced by *Elder's Journal*.

1835-1921	**Lectures on Faith** Removed from *Doctrine in Covenants* in 1921.	
1835-1836	**Joseph Smith's Diary**	
1837	**Elder's Journal** Official church periodical.	
1839-1846	**Times and Seasons** Official church periodical.	
1839-1856	**History of the Church** A seven volume compilation edited by LDS church historian B. H. Roberts.	
1840-1970	**Millennial Star** Official church periodical. Replaced by *Ensign*.	
1842	**Book of Abraham** Joseph Smith's "translation" of Egyptian papyri. Part of the *Pearl of Great Price*.	
1844-1845	**Biographical Sketches of Joseph Smith** Lucy Smith's biography of her son.	
1854-1886	**Journal of Discourses** A collection of 1,438 public sermons given by 55 General Authorities.	
1880	**Pearl of Great Price** Contains excerpts from Joseph's *Inspired Version* and his *Book of Abraham*. Canonized in 1880.	
1887	**An Address to All Believers in Christ** By David Whitmer, Book of Mormon witness.	
1922-1927	**Studies of the Book of Mormon** By B. H. Roberts, LDS church historian and General Authority. Published in 1985.	
1971-present	**Ensign** Official church periodical	

Timeline of key historical events

1805 – Birth

Joseph Smith was born on December 23, 1805, in Sharon, Vermont. He was the fifth of eleven children born to Joseph Smith, Sr. and Lucy Mack Smith.

1820 – First Vision

Joseph claimed that at age 14, in response to praying about which church to join, he was visited by God the Father *and* Jesus Christ, who both appeared to him in human form with bodies of flesh and bone. Joseph claimed he was told not to join any church.

> I was answered that I must join none of them, for they were all wrong; and the Personage who addressed me said that all their creeds were an abomination in his sight; that those professors were all corrupt.
> — Joseph Smith, Mormonism founder

This event is called the *First Vision*. By necessity Mormons believe that an apostasy must have taken place soon after Jesus' apostles died in order for the church Joseph founded to be regarded as the only true Christian church today.

1823 – Angel Moroni

Joseph claimed that at age 17 he was visited by an angel named Moroni, who informed him of an ancient record engraved on gold plates and buried in a nearby hill named Cumorah. Moroni allegedly visited Joseph once a year for five years until 1827, when Joseph was allowed to obtain the plates to translate them.

1827 – Emma Hale

Joseph married his first wife Emma Hale. He would eventually have over 40 wives.

1830 – Book of Mormon / Church of Christ	Joseph published the *Book of Mormon*, his alleged translation of the gold plates, purporting to be "another testament of Jesus Christ". He also founded the *Church of Christ*, later renamed *The Church of Jesus Christ of Latter-day Saints* in 1838.
1844 – Death	The Governor of Illinois had Joseph put in jail for ordering the printing press of a newspaper critical of his church destroyed. An angry mob stormed the jail and killed him along with his brother Hyrum. Joseph's unexpected death created a succession crisis as to who would lead his church.
1847 – Migration to Utah	Those who sided with Brigham Young as Joseph's successor followed him to the Salt Lake basin in Utah.
1852 – Polygamy	Brigham Young, the second and longest serving Mormon prophet, publicly acknowledged the practice of polygamy within the church.
1890 – The Manifesto	Under pressure by the federal government, Wilford Woodruff, the fourth Mormon prophet, issued a manifesto prohibiting the practice of polygamy.
1978 – Priesthood for Blacks	The church lifted its ban on denying blacks its priesthood.
Today	The church has over 14 million members worldwide, with about half in the United States. It operates a global missionary force of 50,000.
	The church claims to be led by continuous revelation from their sitting prophet and twelve apostles.

First Vision

"Joseph Smith's first vision stands today as the greatest event in world history since the birth, ministry, and resurrection of Jesus Christ."

— *LDS.org*

Timeline

Early 1800's	1820	1829	1832, Sept.	1832, Nov.	1835	1842	1880
Visionary tales common throughout New England	First Vision*	Joseph claims to receive Aaronic Priesthood	Joseph: "no man can see God without priesthood"	*Earliest account of the first vision	Diary version	Official version published	Official version canonized

Mormons are taught that local revivals prompted Joseph (age 14) to go into the woods one morning to pray about which church to join. In doing so, Joseph became overwhelmed by a dark force that paralyzed him until God the Father *and* Jesus Christ both appear before him in bodily form. Jesus Christ told Joseph not to join any church as they were all wrong.

If true, this event would be the first ever appearance of God the Father, as the prophets and apostles of biblical times teach us that man has never seen God, nor can see Him.

> You cannot see My face, for no man can see Me and live!
> — *Exodus 33:20*

> No one has seen God at any time; the only begotten God who is in the bosom of the Father, He has explained Him.
> — *John 1:18*

> Not that anyone has seen the Father, except the One who is from God; He has seen the Father.
> — *John 6:46*

> Who alone possesses immortality and dwells in unapproachable light, whom no man has seen or can see…
> — *1 Timothy 6:16*

> No one has seen God at any time…
> — *1 John 4:12*

- This event is the basis for the existence of the Mormon church. For if Joseph was not instructed that all churches were wrong, it nullifies the notion that there was ever a complete apostasy and the notion that the Mormon church is the only true church.
- This event is cited as evidence for the Mormon doctrines that God the Father has a body of flesh and bones and that the Father and Son are separate and distinct gods.

The historicity of this event is doubtful for several reasons:

- There is no evidence for this event but Joseph's own claim.
- He remained silent for over a decade, as the earliest account is twelve years after the visitation allegedly occurred.
- Joseph asserted that priesthood authority is required to see God the Father. He claimed to receive such authority in May of 1829. By his own assertion he could not have seen God the Father nine years prior in 1820.

> And without the ordinances thereof, and the authority of the priesthood, the power of godliness is not manifest unto men in the flesh; For without this no man can see the face of God, even the Father, and live.
> — Joseph Smith, Mormonism founder, *Doctrine and Covenants 84:21-22*

- Visionary tales were common in New England during the early 1800's. Themes in Joseph's own visionary tale appear to be borrowed from other earlier visions.

Contradictory Versions

Versions that predate the church's official version contradict it on key items, including:

- The age when Joseph had the visitation
- His motivation for praying
- Whether or not there were local revivals
- Who appeared before Joseph
- What was and wasn't said to him
- Whether or not he was overwhelmed by a dark force

The three earliest accounts:

- **Official Version (1842)**

    The official version of this event was not published until 1842, over two decades after the vision allegedly occurred. It was canonized in the Pearl of Great Price in 1880.

- **Diary Version (1835)**

    Two entries recorded five days apart in Joseph's diary refer to this event as "a visitation of angels". In this version it is many angels who appear before Joseph.

- **Handwritten Version (1832)**

    The earliest version is a handwritten history written by Joseph. This version is vaulted and has never been formally published by the Mormon church. In this version, Joseph already knew that all churches were wrong before ever going to pray. Only Jesus Christ appears to him.

Version Inconsistencies

	Handwritten Version (1832)	**Diary Version (1835)**	**Official Version (1842)**
Age of visitation	*in the 16th year of my age*	*I was about 14 years old when I received this first communication*	*I was at this time in my fifteenth year*
Local revivals	-	-	Local revivals spark Joseph's curiosity as to which are true and false
Location	-	*I retired to the silent grove*	*I retired to the woods*
Motivation to pray	*by searching the scriptures I found that mankind did not come unto the Lord but they had apostatized from the true and living faith and there was no society or denomination that built upon the gospel of Jesus Christ* Note: here Joseph had already learned for himself that all denominations were wrong.	*looking at the different systems taught the children of men, I knew not who was right or who was wrong and I considered it of the first importance that I should be right*	*My object in going to inquire of the Lord was to know which of all the sects was right, that I might know which to join... <u>for at this time it had never entered into my heart that all were wrong</u>*
Heard noises	-	*I heard a noise behind me like some person walking towards me, I strove again to pray, but could not, the noise of walking seemed to draw nearer, I sprung up on my feet, and looked around, but saw no person or thing that was calculated to produce the noise of walking*	-

Mormon Handbook

Overwhelmed by a dark force	-	-	*immediately I was seized upon by some power which entirely overcame me*
Has difficulty praying	-	*I made a fruitless attempt to pray, my tongue seemed to be swollen in my mouth, so that I could not utter... [after hearing noises] I kneeled down again my mouth was opened and my tongue liberated*	*and [the dark force] had such an astonishing influence over me as to bind my tongue so that I could not speak*
Who appeared	Jesus Christ, implied: *I was crucified for the world*	Many Angels, one testifies about Jesus Christ. Note: Joseph summarized the first encounter as: *the first visitation of angels* and the second encounter with Moroni as: *another vision of angels*	God the Father and Jesus Christ, implied. One introduces the other: *This is My Beloved Son*
Sins forgiven	*I saw the Lord and he spake unto me saying Joseph my son thy sins are forgiven thee*	*he said unto me thy sins are forgiven thee*	-

Full texts

Handwritten Version (1832)

At about the age of twelve years my mind became seriously impressed with regard to the all important concerns for the welfare of my immortal Soul. Which led me to searching the scriptures believing as I was taught that they contained the word of God. Thus applying myself to them and my intimate acquaintance with those of different denominations led me to marvel exceedingly. For I discovered that they did not adorn their profession by a holy walk and Godly conversation agreeable to what I found contained in that sacred depository. This was a grief to my Soul.

Thus from the age of twelve years to fifteen I pondered many things in my heart concerning the situation of the world of mankind; the contentions and divisions; the wickedness and abominations; and the darkness which pervaded the minds of mankind.

My mind became exceedingly distressed for I became convicted of my sins. And by searching the scriptures I found that mankind did not come unto the Lord but that they had apostatized from the true and living faith. And there was no society or denomination that built upon the gospel of Jesus Christ as recorded in the New Testament. And I felt to mourn for my own sins and for the sins of the world.

For I learned in the scriptures that God was the same yesterday, today and forever. That he was no respecter to persons. For he was God. For I looked upon the sun, the glorious luminary of the earth; and also the moon rolling in their majesty through the heavens; and also the stars shining in their courses. And the earth also upon which I stood. And the beast of the field and the fowls of heaven and the fish of the waters. And also man walking forth upon the face of the earth in majesty and in the strength of beauty. Whose power and intelligence in governing the things which are so exceeding great and marvelous even in the likeness of him who created them.

And when I considered upon these things my heart exclaimed well. Hath the wise man said it is a fool that saith in his heart there is no God. My heart exclaimed all these bear testimony and bespeak an omnipotent and omnipresent power: a being who maketh Laws and decreeeth and bindeth all things in their bounds; who filleth Eternity; who was and is and will be from all Eternity to Eternity. And when I considered all these things and that that being seeketh such to worship him as worship him in spirit and in truth: therefore I cried unto the Lord for mercy. For there was none else to whom I could go and to obtain mercy.

And the Lord heard my cry in the wilderness. And while in the attitude of calling upon the Lord, in the 16th year of my age, a pillar of light above the brightness of the sun at noon day come down from above and rested upon me. And I was filled with the spirit of God. And the Lord opened the heavens upon me. And I saw the Lord. And he spake unto me saying, "Joseph my son thy sins are forgiven thee. Go thy way, walk in my statutes and keep my commandments. Behold I am the Lord of glory. I was crucified for the world that all those who believe on my name may have Eternal life. Behold the world lieth in Sin at this time and none doeth good. No not one. They have turned aside from the gospel and keep not my commandments. They draw near to me with their lips while their hearts are far from me and mine anger is kindling against the inhabitants of the earth to visit them according to their ungodliness and to bring to pass that which hath been spoken by the mouth of the prophets and Apostles. Behold and lo I come quickly. As it is written of me in the cloud, clothed in the glory of my Father." And my soul was filled with love and for many days.
— Joseph Smith, *A History of the Life of Joseph Smith*
Note: added punctuation and corrected spelling.

Diary Version (1835)

November 9th entry—Joseph relates his visitation to Joshua, a Jewish minister. This entry was omitted from the History of the Church 2:304.

I commenced giving him [Joshua] a relation of the circumstances connected with the coming forth of the book of Mormon. As follows, being wrought up in my mind respecting the subject of religion and looking at the different systems taught the children of men; I knew not who was right or who was wrong. And I considered it of the first importance that I should be right in matters that involve eternal consequences.

Being thus perplexed in mind I retired to the silent grove and bowed down before the Lord, under a realizing sense that he had said (if the bible be true): ask and you shall receive, knock and it shall be opened, seek and you shall find. And again: if any man lack wisdom let him ask of God who giveth to all men liberally and upbraideth not.

Information was what I most desired at this time. And with a fixed determination to obtain it I called upon the Lord for the first time in the place above stated. Or in other words I made a fruitless attempt to pray. My tongue seemed to be swollen in my mouth so that I could not utter.

I heard a noise behind me like some person walking towards me. I strove again to pray but could not. The noise of walking seemed to draw nearer. I sprung up on my feet and looked around but saw no person or thing that was calculated to produce the noise of walking. I kneeled again. My mouth was opened and my tongue liberated.

And I called on the Lord in mighty prayer. A pillar of fire appeared above my head. It presently rested down upon me and filled me with joy unspeakable. A personage appeared in the midst of this pillar of flame which was spread all around; and yet nothing consumed. Another personage soon appeared like unto the first. He said unto me thy sins are forgiven thee. He testified unto me that Jesus Christ is the Son of God; and I saw many angels in this vision. I was about 14 years old when I received this first communication.

When I was about 17 years old I saw another vision of angels in the night season after I had retired to bed.
— Joseph Smith, Mormonism founder
Note: punctuation added and spelling corrected

November 14th entry—Joseph relates his visitation to Erastus Holmes. The words "visitation of angels" was changed to "first vision" when recorded in the History of the Church 2:312.

A Gentleman called this after noon by the name of Erastus Holmes of Newberry, Clermont County, Ohio. He called to make enquiry about the establishment of the church of the latter-day Saints and to be instructed more perfectly in our doctrine, etc.

I commenced and gave him a brief relation of my experience while in my juvenile years; say from 6 years old up to the time I received the first visitation of Angels; which was when I was about 14 years old. And also the visitations that I received afterward concerning the book of Mormon; and a short account of the rise and progress of the church up to this date. He listened very attentively and seemed highly gratified; and intends to unite with the Church. He is a very candid man. Indeed and I am much pleased with him.
— Joseph Smith, Mormonism founder
Note: punctuation added and spelling corrected

Official Version (1842)

In accordance with this, my determination to ask of God, I retired to the woods to make the attempt. It was on the morning of a beautiful, clear day, early in the spring of eighteen hundred and twenty. It was the first time in my life that I had made such an attempt, for amidst all my anxieties I had never as yet made the attempt to pray vocally.

After I had retired to the place where I had previously designed to go, having looked around me, and finding myself alone, I kneeled down and began to offer up the desires of my heart to God. I had scarcely done so, when immediately I was seized upon by some power which entirely overcame me, and had such an astonishing influence over me as to bind my tongue so that I could not speak. Thick darkness gathered around me, and it seemed to me for a time as if I were doomed to sudden destruction.

But, exerting all my powers to call upon God to deliver me out of the power of this enemy which had seized upon me, and at the very moment when I was ready to sink into despair and abandon myself to destruction—not to an imaginary ruin, but to the power of some actual being from the unseen world, who had such marvelous power as I had never before felt in any being—just at this moment of great alarm, I saw a pillar of light exactly over my head, above the brightness of the sun, which descended gradually until it fell upon me.

It no sooner appeared than I found myself delivered from the enemy which held me bound. When the light rested upon me I saw two Personages, whose brightness and glory defy all description, standing above me in the air. One of them spake unto me, calling me by name and said, pointing to the other—"This is My Beloved Son. Hear Him!"

My object in going to inquire of the Lord was to know which of all the sects was right, that I might know which to join. No sooner, therefore, did I get possession of myself, so as to be able to speak, than I asked the Personages who stood above me in the light, which of all the sects was right (for at this time it had never entered into my heart that all were wrong)—and which I should join.

I was answered that I must join none of them, for they were all wrong; and the Personage who addressed me said that all their creeds were an abomination in his sight; that those professors were all corrupt; that: "they draw near to me with their lips, but their hearts are far from me, they teach for doctrines the commandments of men, having a form of godliness, but they deny the power thereof."

He again forbade me to join with any of them; and many other things did he say unto me, which I cannot write at this time. When I came to myself again, I found myself lying on my back, looking up into heaven. When the light had departed, I had no strength; but soon recovering in some degree, I went home.
— Joseph Smith, Mormonism founder

Conclusion

With no other witnesses to this event, all we have is Joseph's word. But he is not credible when he can't keep his story straight.

If this event were true we would not expect him to wait for over a decade to bring it up.

By suppressing the earliest handwritten version; by omitting in the *History of the Church* the entire November 9th diary entry, and by changing "visitation of angels" to "first vision" in the November 14th diary entry, the Mormon church has presented a consistent version to its members.

First Vision Plagiarized

Joseph Smith's First Vision was not unique to his day, and evidence suggests he plagiarized themes from other tales to fabricate his own visionary tale.

In *The Visionary World of Joseph Smith*, Mormon historian Richard Bushman identified over 33 visionary tales published between 1783 and 1815. The handbook examines six tales that likely provided material for Joseph's visionary tale.

Norris Stearns (1815)

Compare the preface of Stearns's book to Joseph's life story: an illiterate youth; commanded to write a book; a prophet.

> The public are here presented with a book written by an illiterate youth, who has been highly favoured of God, and shown many things, which he is now commanded to write. He earnestly solicits the candid attention of every reader, that it may not stand (as the useless Parenthesis) among the other books of the world; for it is written in obedience to the Divine Command, as a Testimony to show his Calling. Care has been taken, that nothing should be written, but by the immediate command of the Lord; whose Servant and Prophet I am.
> — Norris Stearns, The Religious Experience, preface

The religious sentiment of Stearns's father is similar to Joseph's father.

> My Father was once a praying man, and belonged to the Baptist Church in Leyden; but not having faith in ceremonial ordinances, and dead forms of religion, he withdrew from their meetings, and was soon given up to the buffetings of Satan, that his soul might be saved in the day of our Lord Jesus.
> — Norris Stearns, The Religious Experience, p.5

Comparing the tales

	Norris Stearns (1815)	**Joseph Smith (1842)**
Both near the brink of death	*as I lay apparently upon the brink of eternal woe, seeing nothing but death before me*	*at the very moment when I was ready to sink into despair and abandon myself to destruction*
Both are interrupted by light	*there appeared a small gleam of light in the room above the brightness of the sun*	*I saw a pillar of light exactly over my head above the brightness of the sun*
Both see the Father and the Son in bodily form	*I saw two spirits... One was God my maker, almost in bodily shape like a man... below him stood Jesus Christ my Redeemer, in perfect shape like a man...*	*I saw two personages... standing above me in the air. One of them spake unto me, calling me by name and said, pointing to the other - This is My Beloved Son.*
Both struggle to describe the appearance	*I could not describe their glory*	*whose brightness and glory defy all description*
Both use "pillar" in their descriptions	*a Pillar and a Cloud*	*a pillar of light*

Elias Smith (1816)

	Elias Smith (1816)	**Joseph Smith (1842)**
Both enter the woods in the morning	*I went into the woods one morning*	*I retired to the woods to make the attempt. It was on the morning of a beautiful, clear day*
Both see a light	*a light appeared to shine from heaven*	*I saw a pillar of light exactly over my head*
Both have a divine encounter	*My mind seemed to rise in that light to the throne of God and the Lamb, and while thus gloriously led... And I looked, and, lo, a Lamb stood on the mount Sion*	*When the light rested on me I saw two Personages, whose brightness and glory defy all description*

Solomon Chamberlain (1816)

Chamberlain visited Palmyra and met with the Smith family in the fall of 1829. He eventually joined the Mormon church.

	Solomon Chamberlain (1816)	**Joseph Smith (1842)**
Both prayed about denominational concerns and were answered that all were corrupt	*the angel had made known to me in the vision, that all Churches and Denominations on the earth had became corrupt*	*I was answered that I must join none of them, for they were all wrong... all their creeds were an abomination in his sight; that those professors were all corrupt*

Charles Finney (1821)

Finney visited Joseph Smith's community in 1831.

	Charles Finney (1821)	**Joseph Smith (1842)**
Both are impressed with scripture	*Just at that point this passage of Scripture seemed to drop into my mind with a flood of light... I instantly seized hold of this with my heart*	*Never did any passage of scripture come with more power to the heart of man than this did at this time to mine. It seemed to enter with great force into every feeling of my heart*
Both enter the woods to be alone to pray	*I turned and bent my course toward the woods, feeling that I must be alone, and away from all human eyes and ears, so that I could pour out my prayers to God... I crept into this place and knelt down for prayer*	*I retired to the woods to make the attempt... having looked around me, and finding myself alone, I kneeled down and began to offer up the desires of my heart to God*
Both struggle to pray	*But when I attempted to pray I found that my heart would not pray... But lo! when I came to try, I was dumb; that is, I had nothing to say to God; or at least I could say but a few words*	*It was the first time in my life that I had made such an attempt, for amidst all my anxieties I had never as yet made the attempt to pray vocally... I was seized upon by some power... and had such an astonishing influence over me as to bind my tongue so I could not speak*

Both overwhelmed by power	*An overwhelming sense of my wickedness in being ashamed to have a human being see me on my knees before God, took such powerful possession of me*	*When immediately I was seized upon by some power which entirely overcame me, and had such an astonishing influence over me*
Both fall into despair	*Finally I found myself verging fast to despair*	*at the very moment when I was ready to sink into despair*
Both experience weakness	*I felt almost too weak to stand upon my knees*	*I had no strength; but soon recovering some degree*

Asa Wild (1823)

	Asa Wild (1823)	**Joseph Smith (1842)**
Both have a divine encounter	*realizing in a remarkable manner the majesty, greatness and glory, of that Being*	*I saw two Personages, whose brightness and glory defy all description*
Both lose capacity	*It seemed as if my mind, though active in its very nature, had lost all its activity, and was struck motionless, as well as into nothing*	*When immediately I was seized upon by some power which entirely overcame me, and had such an astonishing influence over me as to bind my tongue so that I could not speak*
Both are told all denominations are corrupt	*He also told me, that every denomination of professing christians had become extremely corrupt*	*the Personages who addressed me said that all their creeds were an abomination in his sight; that those professors were all corrupt*
Both withhold additional information	*and many other things did he say unto me, which I cannot write at this time*	*Much more the Lord revealed, but forbids my relating it in this way*

James Marsh (1838)

BYU professor and Mormon historian D. Michael Quinn's summary:

> 7 May, 1838. James G. Marsh, 14-year-old son of the president of the Quorum of Twelve, dies. The Elder's Journal issue of July notes that at age nine this boy 'had a remarkable vision, in which he talked with the Father and many of the ancient prophets face to face, and beheld the Son of God coming in his glory.' No publication at this time had yet referred to Smith's vision of the Father and the Son.
>
> — *The Mormon Hierarchy: Origins of Power, p.628*

The obituary in the Elder's Journal was written just before the official version was composed.

	Marsh's Obituary (1838)	**Joseph Smith (1842)**
Both are visited by the Father and Son	*he talked with God the Father and many of the ancient prophets face to face, and beheld the Son of God coming in his glory*	*I saw two Personages, whose brightness and glory defy all description... One of them spake unto me... This is My Beloved Son.*
Both use similar phrasing for dating	*early in the spring of 1832*	*early in the spring of [1820]*

Full Texts

Norris Stearns (1815)

At length, as I lay apparently upon the brink of eternal woe, seeing nothing but death before me, suddenly there came a sweet flow of the love of God to my soul, which gradually increased. At the same time, there appeared a small gleam of light in the room, above the brightness of the sun, then at his meridian, which grew brighter and brighter: As this light and love increased, my sins began to separate, and the Mountain removed towards the east. At length, being in an ecstasy of joy, I turned to the other side of the bed, (whether in the body or out I cannot tell, God knoweth) there I saw two spirits, which I knew at the first sight. But if I had the tongue of an Angel I could not

describe their glory, for they brought the joys of heaven with them. One was God, my Maker, almost in bodily shape like a man. His face was, as it were a flame of Fire, and his body, as it had been a Pillar and a Cloud. In looking steadfastly to discern features, I could see none, but a small glimpse would appear in some other place. Below him stood Jesus Christ my Redeemer, in perfect shape like a man—His face was not ablaze, but had the countenance of fire, being bright and shining. His Father's will appeared to be his! All was condescension, peace, and love!!
— Norris Stearns, *The Religious Experience,* as quoted in *The Visionary World of Joseph Smith*

Elias Smith (1816)

Not long after these things passed through my mind, I went into the woods one morning after a stick of timber; after taking it on my shoulder to bring it to the house, as I walked along on large log that lay above the snow, my foot slipped and I fell partly under the log, the timber fell one end on the log and the other on the snow, and held me, as that I found it difficult at first to rise from the situation I was then in. While in this situation, a light appeared to shine from heaven, not only into my head, but into my heart. This was something very strange to me, and what I had never experienced before. My mind seemed to rise in that light to the throne of God and the Lamb, and while thus gloriously led, what appeared to my understanding was expressed in Rev. xiv. 1. "And I looked, and, lo, a Lamb stood on the mount Sion, and with him an hundred forty and four thousand, having his Father's name written in their foreheads." The Lamb once slain appeared to my understanding, and while viewing him, I felt such love to him as I never felt to any thing earthly. My mind was calm and at peace with God through the Lamb of God, that taketh away the sin of the world. The view of the Lamb on mount Sion gave my joy unspeakable and full of glory. It is not possible for me to tell how long I remained in that situation, as every thing earthly was gone from me for some time.
— Elias Smith, *The Life, Conversion, Preaching, Travel, and Sufferings of Elias Smith, pp.58-59*

Solomon Chamberlain (1816)

[I] found Hyrum walking the floor, As I entered the door, I said, peace be to this house. He looked at me as one astonished, and said, I hope it will be peace, I then said, Is there any one here that believes in visions or revelations and he said Yes, we are a visionary house. I said, Then I will give you one of my pamphlets, which was visionary, and of my own experience. They then called the people together, which consisted of five or six men who were out at the door. Father Smith was one and some of the Whitmer's. Then they sat down and read my pamphlet. Hyrum read first, but was so affected he could not read it. He then gave it to a man, which I learned was Christian Whitmer, he finished reading it. I then opened my mouth and began to preach to them, in the words that the angel had made known to me in the vision, that all Churches and Denominations on the earth had become corrupt, and no Church of God on the earth buy that he would shortly rise up a Church, that would never be confounded nor brought down and be like unto the Apostolic Church. They wondered greatly who had been telling me these things, for said they we have the same things wrote down in our house, taken from the Gold record, that you are preaching to us. I said, the Lord told me these things a number of years ago, I then said, If you are a visionary house, I wish you would make known some of your discoveries, for I think I can bear them.

— Solomon Chamberlain, *A Short Sketch of the Life of Solomon Chamberlain*, as quoted in *The Visionary World of Joseph Smith*

Charles Finney (1821)

North of the village, and over a hill, lay a piece of woods, in which I was in the almost daily habit of walking, more or less, when it was pleasant weather. It was now October, and the time was past for my frequent walks there. Nevertheless, instead of going to the office, I turned and bent my course toward the woods, feeling that I must be alone, and away from all human eyes and ears, so that I could pour out my prayer to God.

But still my pride must show itself. As I went over the hill, it occurred to me that someone might see me and suppose that I was going away to pray. Yet probably there was not a person on earth that would have suspected such a thing, had he seen me going. But so great was my pride, and so much was I possessed with the fear of man, that I recollect that I skulked along under the fence, till I got so far out of sight that no one from the village could see me. I then penetrated into the woods, I should think, a quarter of a mile, went over on the other side of the hill, and found a place where some large trees had fallen across each other, leaving an open place between. There I saw I could make a kind of closet. I crept into this place and knelt down for prayer. As I turned to go up into the woods, I recollect to have said, "I will give my heart to God, or I never will come down from there." I recollect repeating this as I went up: "I will give my heart to God before I ever come down again."

But when I attempted to pray I found that my heart would not pray. I had supposed that if I could only be where I could speak aloud, without being overheard, I could pray freely. But lo! when I came to try, I was dumb; that is, I had nothing to say to God; or at least I could say but a few words, and those without heart. In attempting to pray I would hear a rustling in the leaves, as I thought, and would stop and look up to see if somebody were not coming. This I did several times.

Finally I found myself verging fast to despair. I said to myself, "I cannot pray. My heart is dead to God, and will not pray." I then reproached myself for having promised to give my heart to God before I left the woods. When I came to try, I found I could not give my heart to God. My inward soul hung back, and there was no going out of my heart to God. I began to feel deeply that it was too late; that it must be that I was given up of God and was past hope.

The thought was pressing me of the rashness of my promise, that I would give my heart to God that day or die in the attempt. It seemed to me as if that was binding upon my soul; and yet I was going to break my vow. A great sinking and discouragement came over me, and I felt almost too weak to stand upon my knees.

Just at this moment I again thought I heard someone approach me, and I opened my eyes to see whether it were so. But right there the revelation of my pride of heart, as the great difficulty that stood in the way, was distinctly shown to me. An overwhelming sense of my wickedness in being ashamed to have a human being see me on my knees before God, took such powerful possession of me, that I cried at the top of my voice, and exclaimed that I would not leave that place if all the men on earth and all the devils in hell surrounded me. "What!" I said, "such a degraded sinner I am, on my knees confessing my sins to the great and holy God; and ashamed to have any human being, and a sinner like myself, find me on my knees endeavoring to make my peace with my offended God!" The sin appeared awful, infinite. It broke me down before the Lord.

Just at that point this passage of Scripture seemed to drop into my mind with a flood of light: "Then shall ye go and pray unto me, and I will hearken unto you. Then shall ye seek me and find me, when ye shall search for me with all your heart." I instantly seized hold of this with my heart. I had intellectually believed the Bible before; but never had the truth been in my mind that faith was a voluntary trust instead of an intellectual state. I was as conscious as I was of my existence, of trusting at that moment in God's veracity. Somehow I knew that that was a passage of Scripture, though I do not think I had ever read it. I knew that it was God's word, and God's voice, as it were, that spoke to me. I cried to Him, "Lord, I take Thee at Thy word. Now Thou knowest that I do search for Thee with all my heart, and that I have come here to pray to Thee; and Thou hast promised to hear me.
— Charles Finney, *Memoirs of Revival of Religion, Ch. 2*

Asa Wild (1823)

Asa Wild Remarkable Vision and Revelation:
as seen and received by Asa Wild, of Amsterdam, (N. Y.)

Having a number of months enjoyed an unusual degree of the light of God's countenance, and having been much favoured of the Lord in many respects, and after having enjoyed the sweetest, and most ravishing communions with Him; the Lord in his boundless goodness was pleased to communicate the following Revelation, having in the first place presented me with a very glorious Vision, in which I saw the same things:

In the first place I observe that my mind had been brought into the most profound stillness, and awe; realizing in a remarkable manner the majesty, greatness and glory, of that Being before whom all nations are as the drop of the bucket. It seemed as if my mind, though active in its very nature, had lost all its activity, and was struck motionless, as well as into nothing, before the awful and glorious majesty of the Great Jehovah. He then spake to the following ourport; and in such a manner as I could not describe if I should attempt. -- He told me that the Millennium state of the world is about to take place; that in seven years literally, there would scarce a sinner be found on earth; that the earth itself, as well as the souls and bodies of its inhabitants, should be redeemed, as before the fall, and become as the garden of Eden. He told me that all of the most dreadful and terrible judgments spoken in the blessed scriptures were to be executed within that time, that more than two thirds of the inhabitants of the world would be destroyed by these judgments; some of which are the following -- wars, massacres, famine, pestilence, earthquakes, civil, political and ecclesiastical commotions; and above all, various and dreadful judgments executed immediately by God, through the instrumentality of the Ministers of the Millennial dispensation which is to exceed in glory every other dispensation; a short description of which may be seen in the last chapter of Isaiah, and in other places. He also told me, that every denomination of professing christians had become extremely corrupt; many of which had never had any true faith at all; but are guided only by depraved reason, refusing the teaching of the spirit [illegible lines]... which alone can teach us the true meaning [illegible lines]... He told me further, that he had raised up, and was now raising up, that class of persons signified by the angel mentioned by the Revelator XIV. 6, 7, which flew in the midst of heaven; having the everlasting gospel to preach, that these persons are of an inferior [social] class, and small learning; that they were rejected by every denomination as a body; but soon, God will open their way, by miracles, judgments, &c. that they will have higher authority, greater power, superior inspiration, and a greater degree of holiness than was ever experienced before [illegible lines] ... divine grace and glory

Furthermore he said that all the different denominations of professing christians constituted the New Testament Babylon; and that he should deal with them according to what is written of IT, in the book of Revelation: that he is about to call out all his sincere children who are mourning in Zion, from oppression and tyranny of the mother of harlots; and that the severest judgments will be inflicted on the professors of religion; which will immediately commence in Amsterdam, and has already commenced in different parts of the world, and even in this country. And though their operations at first are gradual, and under cover, yet it will soon be generally seen that it is the immediate execution of divine vengeance upon an ungodly world.

Much more the Lord revealed, but forbids my relating it in this way. But this, I have written and published, by the express and immediate command of God: the truth and reality of which, I know with the most absolute certainty. -- Though I have ever been the most backward to believe things of this nature; having been brought up in the Calvinistic system, and having had a thorough understanding of the same, and was fully established in the belief of it for several years after I experienced the love of God in my heart: but finding the Calvinists did not understand the glorious depths of holiness, and conformity to the divine character in heart and practice, which I saw was our privilege and duty I joined the Methodist Church, which I found had much clearer and more scriptural views on these and some other points than the Calvinists; though I soon saw that they as a body, were very corrupt, having departed much from their primitive purity and holiness. I also saw that their first founders did not travel into all that was their privilege; and that vastly greater depths of holiness might have been experienced even by them. Yet I thank God for what light I have received through their instrumentality, but know that much greater and more glorious light is about to burst upon the world."
Amsterdam, October, 1823.
— Asa Wild, *Wayne Sentinel, Palmyra, New York, October 22, 1823*

James G. Marsh Vision (1838)

OBITUARY.

DIED on the 7th of May last, James G. Marsh, second son of Thomas B. Marsh, aged 14 years, 11 months and seven days.

From early infancy he manifested a love and reverence towards his Heavenly Father, while his parents diligently taught him the first principles of the gospel of Jesus Christ. And having a thirst for knowledge and a love of good principles, he eagerly embraced the gospel, and was baptized into the Church of Jesus Christ of latter day saints, early in the spring of 1832, being between eight and nine years of age.

His great love of knowledge led him to take hold of every opportunity to read the most useful books, and as he was a lover of the gospel, he made himself well acquainted with the sacred writings, and even at this early age, he had become well skilled in profane as well as sacred history.

It seems that the Lord had respect unto this lover of righteousness, for when he was but about nine years of age, he had a remarkable vision, in which he talked with the Father and many of the ancient prophets face to face, and beheld the Son of God coming in his glory.
— *Elder's Journal, Vol. 1, No. 3, p.48*

Conclusion

Either God was trying to restore the true Christian church to dozens throughout New England or Joseph's tale is a copy-cat among many.

Apostasy

"I will come out on the top at last. I have more to boast of than ever any man had. I am the only man that has ever been able to keep a whole church together since the days of Adam. A large majority of the whole have stood by me. Neither Paul, John, Peter, nor Jesus ever did it. I boast that no man ever did such a work as I. The followers of Jesus ran away from Him; but the Latter-day Saints never ran away from me yet."
— Joseph Smith

The Church of Jesus Christ of Latter-day Saints claims to be the only true Christian church. This comes from Joseph Smith's *First Vision* where he was allegedly informed that all churches were corrupt. For this to be true, it requires that sometime after Jesus Christ founded his church it went into complete apostasy.

> Nothing less than a complete apostasy from the Christian religion would warrant the establishment of the Church of Jesus Christ of Latter-day Saints.
> — B. H. Roberts, LDS church historian, *History of the Church, vol. 1, p.XLII*

> If the alleged apostasy of the primitive church was not a reality, the church of Jesus Christ of Latter-day Saints is not the divine institution its name proclaims.
> — James Talmage, Mormon apostle, *The Great Apostasy, preface*

Since Mormonism claims to be restored Christianity, it assumes that it is identical today to the church Jesus Christ founded. Mormons also assume, by necessity, that where mainstream Christian doctrine and biblical scripture differ, it is the result of corruption.

But if men through apostasy had corrupted the Christian religion and lost divine authority to administer the ordinances of the Gospel, it was of the utmost importance that a new dispensation of the true Christian religion should be given to the world.
— B. H. Roberts, LDS church historian, *History of the Church, vol. 1, p.XLII*

Condemning Christianity

Mormon prophets have voiced their disdain for the rest of Christianity.

Are Christians ignorant? Yes, as ignorant of the things of God as the brute beast.
— John Taylor, Mormon prophet, *Journal of Discourses 6:25*

The Christian world, so called, are heathens as to their knowledge of the salvation of God.
— Brigham Young, Mormon prophet, *Journal of Discourses 8:171*

With regard to true theology, a more ignorant people never lived than the present so-called Christian world.
— Brigham Young, Mormon prophet, *Journal of Discourses 8:199*

What does the Christian world know about God? Nothing; yet these very men assume the right and power to tell others what they shall and what they shall not believe in. Why, so far as the things of God are concerned, they are the veriest fools; they know neither God nor the things of God.
— John Taylor, Mormon prophet, *Journal of Discourses 13:225*

Condemning the Catholic Church

The Book of Mormon speaks of an "abominable church" that is the "whore of all the earth" founded by the devil. This church allegedly removed "plain and precious" truths from the Bible. 1 Nephi 13:5,6,8,32,34; 13:26,28; 14:3,9,15,17; 22:13,14; 2 Nephi 6:12; 28:18

General authorities have identified this abominable church as the Catholic church.

> It is also to the Book of Mormon to which we turn for the plainest description of the Catholic Church as the great and abominable church. Nephi saw this 'church which is the most abominable above all other churches' in vision. He 'saw the devil that he was the foundation of it' and also the murders, wealth, harlotry, persecutions, and evil desires that historically have been a part of this satanic organization.
> — Bruce McConkie, Mormon apostle, *Mormon Doctrine, p.130 1958*

> Who founded the Roman Catholic Church? The Devil, through the medium of Apostates.
> — Orson Pratt, Mormon apostle, *The Seer, p.205*

The Mormon church has backed away from these statements. After authorizing Orson Pratt to publish *The Seer* in 1853, it later condemned unidentified portions of it twelve years later. The church also forced Bruce McConkie to republish a softer toned *Mormon Doctrine*. However the question remains: if not the Catholic church, what then is the "abominable church" in the Book of Mormon?

Distrust of the Bible

While the *King James Version* is part of the LDS canon of scripture, Mormons generally regard it as less authoritative than other Mormon scripture. Whenever the Bible is silent or contradicts modern LDS doctrine, Mormons consider it a result of corruption during the alleged apostasy.

- The Book of Mormon says that an abominable church removed plain and precious truths from the Bible.

  > Wherefore, thou seest that after the book hath gone forth through the hands of the great and abominable church, that there are many plain and precious things taken away from the book, which is the book of the Lamb of God. v.28

  > ...because of the plain and most precious parts of the gospel of the Lamb which have been kept back by that abominable church, whose formation thou hast seen. v.32
  > — *1 Nephi 13:28,32*

- This second rate treatment is evidenced in the eighth Article of Faith.

  > We believe the Bible to be the word of God as far as it is translated correctly; we also believe the Book of Mormon to be the word of God.
  > — Joseph Smith, Mormonism founder, *Article of Faith, #8*

- The biblical texts were originally written in Hebrew, Aramaic and Greek. That there are minor errors in English translations is a given. The burden is on the Mormon church to prove where any error has resulted in corrupted doctrine.

- That Joseph performed his own translation of the Bible, called the *Inspired Version*, complicates the Mormon allegation that the Bible has not been translated correctly.

  > The Joseph Smith Translation, or Inspired Version, is a thousand times over the best Bible now existing on earth.
  > — Bruce McConkie, Mormon apostle, *Ensign, June, 1999*

The Book of Mormon spared the apostasy

The Book of Mormon should have been spared corruption from any alleged apostasy as it was supposedly buried for 1,406 years. Therefore we should expect it to contain pure Christian doctrine. However the Book of Mormon mostly echoes the teachings in the Bible.

The Book of Mormon is silent on the peculiar doctrines that separate Mormonism from Christianity, including:

- Aaronic priesthood
- Baptisms for the dead
- Celestial marriage
- Church organization
- Exaltation
- Polytheism
- Three heavens

An Apostle and Three Disciples

LDS scripture contradicts the allegation that Christianity suffered a complete apostasy.

- Book of Mormon, 3 Nephi 28 says that three disciples would not die so they could preach the gospel until the second coming of Jesus Christ.
- Doctrine and Covenants, Section 7 says that Apostle John would not die so he could preach the gospel until the second coming of Jesus Christ.

Conclusion

Jesus Christ made several promises that give us assurance that an apostasy never took place.

> Upon this rock I will build My church; and the gates of Hades will not overpower it.
> — *Matthew 16:18*

> Go therefore and make disciples of all the nations, baptizing them in the name of the Father and the Son and the Holy Spirit, teaching them to observe all that I commanded you; and lo, I am with you always, even to the end of the age.
> — *Matthew 28:19-20*

> I will ask the Father, and He will give you another Helper, that He may be with you forever.
> — *John 14:16*

Succession Crisis

Joseph Smith's unexpected death created a crisis as to who would lead the church. Several assumed power which caused the church to split. Some of the more notable movements include:

James Strang

Claiming that Joseph said he would be the successor, some followed elder James Strang, including three apostles, eight Book of Mormon witnesses, and Joseph's mother Lucy Smith. Like Joseph Smith, Strang claimed to have also translated plates. This movement exists today as the *Church of Jesus Christ of Latter Day Saints*.

Sidney Rigdon

Some followed Sidney Rigdon, who was Joseph's *First Counselor*. William Bickerton continued this movement which exists today as the *Church of Jesus Christ*.

Joseph Smith III

Some believed that Joseph's son, Joseph Smith III, should be his successor. This movement became the *Reorganized Church of Jesus Christ of Latter Day Saints*. In 2001 it was renamed to *Community of Christ*.

Brigham Young

Some followed senior apostle Brigham Young, who migrated his followers to Utah. This movement has grown to become the largest, claiming a global membership of 14 million. It is this organization, *The Church of Jesus Christ of Latter-day Saints*, that is the focus of this handbook.

Granville Hedrick

Various smaller groups split after Joseph's death. In 1863 five branches along with John E. Page, an apostle under Joseph Smith, united under the leadership of Granville Hedrick. This church owns the temple lot spoken of in Joseph Smith's New Jerusalem prophecy.

David Whitmer

David Whitmer was one of the Book of Mormon's three witnesses. On July 7, 1834, when Joseph Smith ordained Whitmer as the president of the Missouri church, he also named Whitmer his successor. After Joseph's death, Whitmer formed a church (Church of Christ) to accommodate those disillusioned with Sidney Rigdon, which included Mormon apostle William E. M'Lellin and Mormon *Seventy* Benjamin Winchester. This church dissolved in the 1960s.

General Authorities

The LDS church claims to be led by modern revelation by the sitting Mormon prophet. Yet few Mormon prophets have given "revelation" since Joseph Smith.

The LDS church is structured as a vertical hierarchy that employs a chain of command from the prophet, who also serves as the organization's president, down to priesthood for boys as young as twelve.

Quotes in this handbook are from *General Authorities*—those who hold or have held offices in the top three tiers.

First Presidency

The prophet is also the president of the church. He appoints two counselors, which together comprise the *First Presidency*. The prophet serves for life, and upon his death is replaced by the longest serving apostle.

Quorum of Twelve

Twelve apostles serve life terms, and may be appointed to the *First Presidency*, either upon death of the prophet, or appointed as one of his counselors. Together with the *First Presidency* they conduct church policy and administration.

Quorum of Seventy

The *Seventy* serve as regional presidents throughout the world. There are two quorums: the *First Quorum* serve lifetime appointments. The *Second Quorum* serve about five to seven years. Seven men are appointed from both quorums to the *Presidency of the Seventy*.

Christian (New Testament) Organization

The apostles and prophets of Biblical times teach that the office of prophet (not to be confused with the gift of prophecy—1 Cor. 14:1) was superseded by Jesus Christ.

> In the past God spoke to our ancestors through the prophets at many times and in various ways, but in these last days he has spoken to us by his Son…
> — *Hebrews 1:2*

The authority of Jesus Christ's apostles supersedes all other offices including prophets.

> In the church God has appointed <u>first</u> apostles, <u>second</u> prophets, third teachers…
> — *1 Corinthians 12:28*

The prophets and apostles of Biblical times are the foundation of the Christian church, which work is complete.

> Having been built on the foundation of the apostles and prophets, Christ Jesus himself as the chief corner stone.
> — *Ephesians 2:20*

The Canon

What constitutes official scripture in the Mormon church has evolved over the years. The following is the official LDS canon today, also called the *Standard Works*.

- Book of Mormon
- Doctrine & Covenants
- Pearl of Great Price
- King James Version Bible

Book of Mormon

The Book of Mormon narrative follows the journey of ancient Jews who migrate and settle the New World, culminating in the resurrected Jesus Christ visiting the inhabitants of the Americas.

- According to the narrative the first migration (Jaredites) occurred around the time of the Tower of Babel (2500 BC).
- The second group to migrate were the Nephites in 600 BC, followed shortly thereafter by the Mulekites. When the Mulekites arrived the Jaredites were extinct.
- The bulk of the Book of Mormon follows the Nephites as they settle the Americas. The unrighteous (Lamanites) are cursed with dark skin, and split from the Nephites. By 421 AD, the Lamanites exterminated all of the Nephites.
- Mormons believe that Native Indians are the ancestors of the Lamanites.
- The Book of Mormon claims that the truthfulness of its narrative can be determined not by analysis but by prayer.

Book of Mormon Origins

"I told the brethren that the Book of Mormon was the most correct of any book on earth, and the keystone of our religion, and a man would get nearer to God by abiding by its precepts, than by any other book."
— Joseph Smith

Timeline

1823	1827	1828	1830
Joseph is visited by the angel Moroni who informs him of a buried book engraved on gold plates	Joseph obtains the gold plates to translate them	The first 116 pages of the translation are lost	Joseph's translation is published as the *Book of Mormon*

Joseph Smith claimed that three years after he received the First Vision, he had another visitation, this time by an angel named Moroni:

> He said there was a book deposited, written upon gold plates, giving an account of the former inhabitants of this continent, and the source from whence they sprang. He also said that the fullness of the everlasting Gospel was contained in it, as delivered by the Savior to the ancient inhabitants.
> — Joseph Smith, Mormonism founder, *Joseph Smith History 1:64*

- The angel Moroni allegedly visited Joseph once a year for five years until 1827, when Joseph was allowed to obtain the gold plates and translate them.
- The language on the plates is called *reformed Egyptian*—unknown today.
- Joseph Smith gave Martin Harris (a friend interested in financing the translation) a paper with characters allegedly copied from the gold plates so that Harris could get an independent opinion of them.

- Martin Harris took home the first 116 pages of Joseph's translation to show to his wife, as she was skeptical of the project and concerned that Harris was being financially gullible. The manuscript came up missing.
- Unfortunately we are unable to view the gold plates today, as according to Joseph, the angel Moroni took them back after Joseph had completed his translation. Joseph enlisted witnesses to provide testimony that they saw the gold plates.

Gold Plates

Joseph Smith claimed that his Book of Mormon is his translation of an ancient book engraved on gold plates that he found buried in a hill.

Language

The language on the plates is called *reformed Egyptian*—an unknown language.

Dimensions

According to Joseph, the book was 6" x 8" x 6" and each plate was thinner than "common tin".

> Each plate was six inches wide and eight inches long and not quite so thick as common tin. They were filled with engravings, in Egyptian characters and bound together in a volume, as the leaves of a book with three rings running through the whole. The volume was something near six inches in thickness, a part of which was sealed.
> — Joseph Smith, Mormonism founder, *Times and Seasons, 3:707*

The Sealed Portion

Two witnesses said that 2/3 of the book was sealed, leaving 1/3 (2 inches) of translatable plates.

- David Whitmer, Mormon apostle, *Chicago Times, October 17, 1881*
- Orson Pratt, Mormon apostle, *Journal of Discourses 3:347*

Weight

The weight of plates range from 30 to 60 pounds.

Name	Weight
Joseph Smith Sr. (Joseph's father) *Interview, Historical Magazine, 7:307*	30 lbs
Martin Harris, Mormon apostle *Interview, Tiffany's Monthly, August 1859, p.166*	40-50 lbs
William Smith (Joseph's brother) *William Smith on Mormonism, p.12*	60 lbs

Running with the plates

In another of Joseph's tales, of which again he is the only witness, he claims that he was assaulted by several men while bringing the gold plates home. Somehow he was able to outrun them while carrying the 30-60 pound plates. This despite lifelong complications from leg surgery. After hearing Joseph's tale a group went out to find these men but had no success.

- Joseph's childhood surgery

> Joseph, who was about seven years old, developed a serious infection in his left leg. Dr. Nathan Smith of Dartmouth Medical School at nearby Hanover, New Hampshire, agreed to perform a new surgical procedure to try to save the boy's leg... Joseph bravely endured as the surgeon bored into and chipped away part of his leg bone. The surgery was successful, although Joseph walked the next several years with crutches and showed signs of a slight limp the rest of his life.
> — *Teachings of the Presidents of the Church, xxii-25*

- Joseph's mother recorded Joseph's story

    The plates were secreted about three miles from home... Joseph, on coming to them, took them from their secret place, and, wrapping them in his linen frock, placed them under his arm and started for home.

    After proceeding a short distance, he thought it would be more safe to leave the road and go through the woods. Traveling some distance after he left the road, he came to a large windfall, and as he was jumping over a log, a man sprang up from behind it, and gave him a heavy blow with a gun. Joseph turned around and knocked him down, then ran at the top of his speed. About half a mile further he was attacked again in the same manner as before; he knocked this man down in like manner as the former, then ran on again; and before he reached home he was assaulted the third time...

    I will here mention that my husband, Mr. Knight, and Mr. Stoal, went in pursuit of those villains who had attempted Joseph's life, but were not able to find them.
    — Lucy Smith, *Biographical Sketches of Joseph Smith, ch.23*

- Joseph's friend Willard Chase recalled the story told by Joseph

    [Joseph] went for his book, found it safe, took off his frock, wrapt it round it, put it under his arm and ran all the way home, a distance of about two miles. He said he should think it would weigh sixty pounds, and was sure it would weigh forty. On his return home, he said he was attacked by two men in the woods, and knocked them both down and made his escape, arrived safe and secured his treasure.
    — William Chase, *Mormonism Unvailed, p.246*

Book of Mormon Witnesses

The Book of Mormon contains two sets of joint statements written by Joseph Smith for those who claimed to have seen the gold plates to sign.

Three Witnesses

The Three Witnesses are David Whitmer, Oliver Cowdery, and Martin Harris—who mortgaged his farm to finance the first printing of the Book of Mormon.

It is inconclusive if the witnesses actually saw plates or if they only claimed to see them through a visionary experience. The testimony published in the Book of Mormon suggests it was through supernatural means:

> And we also testify that we have seen the engravings which are upon the plates; and they have been shown unto us by the power of God, and not of man. And we declare with words of soberness, that an angel of God came down from heaven, and he brought and laid before our eyes, that we beheld and saw the plates, and the engravings thereon.
> — Oliver Cowdery, David Whitmer, Martin Harris, *The Testimony of Three Witnesses*

Since all three served as scribes for Joseph as he dictated the Book of Mormon, it is perplexing why an angel would need to come down and show them the plates.

Eight Witnesses

The Book of Mormon also includes a joint statement for eight men who claim to have seen the gold plates. It's important to note that:

- Half of the witnesses are related to David Whitmer.
- Three are related to Joseph Smith including his father and two brothers.

Fallout

The relationship with the witnesses was strained.

> Some of the witnesses of the Book of Mormon, who handled the plates and conversed with the angels of God, were afterwards left to doubt and to disbelieve that they had ever seen an angel.*
> — Brigham Young, Mormon prophet, *Journal of Discourses 7:164*
> * Notice Brigham equates seeing the plates with seeing an angel

- Within eight years all of the Three Witnesses were excommunicated from the church.

> Such characters as McLellin, John Whitmer, David Whitmer, Oliver Cowdery, and Martin Harris, are too mean to mention; and we had liked to have forgotten them.
> — Joseph Smith, Mormonism founder, *History of the Church 3:232*

- After Joseph Smith's death, Oliver Cowdery eventually joined the Methodist church. Martin Harris and David Whitmer followed James Strang.

Conclusion

In the end, whatever the witnesses saw or claimed to have seen through a vision doesn't matter, because none could read reformed Egyptian, so none could independently verify that Joseph's Book of Mormon is an accurate translation.

Book of Mormon Translation

Joseph Smith claimed that the Book of Mormon is his translation of an ancient book engraved on gold plates.

Ironically, according to eyewitnesses, Joseph did not look at the plates while "translating" them.

> I will now give you a description of the manner in which the Book of Mormon was translated. Joseph Smith would put the seer stone into a hat, and put his face in the hat, drawing it closely around his face to exclude the light; and in the darkness the spiritual light would shine. A piece of something resembling a parchment would appear, and on that appeared the writing. Once character at a time would appear, and under it was the interpretation in English. Brother Joseph would read off the English to Oliver Cowdery, who was his principle scribe, and when it was written down and repeated to Brother Joseph to see if it was correct, then it would disappear, and another character with the interpretation would appear.
> — David Whitmer, Mormon apostle, *An Address to All Believers in Christ, p.12*

> In writing for your father I frequently wrote day after day, often sitting at the table close by him, he sitting with his face buried in his hat, with the stone in it, and dictating hour after hour with nothing between us.
> — Emma Smith, Joseph Smith's wife, *Interview with her son Joseph Smith III, The Saints Herald, Vol. 26, No. 19, p.289*

Urim and Thummim

The Mormon church emphasizes that Joseph used an ancient device called the Urim and Thummim to aid with his translation.

The Urim and Thummim are not to be confused with the seer stone.

> There were a couple of means that were prepared for this. One was that he used an instrument that was found with the plates that was called the Urim and Thummim. This is kind of a divinatory device that goes back into Old Testament times. Actually, most of the translation was done using something called a seer stone. The seer stone is obviously something like the Urim and Thummim. It seems to be a stone that was found in the vicinity, and I can't say exactly how it would have worked. It may have been a kind of a concentrating device or a device to facilitate concentration. He would put the stone for most of the concentration period in the bottom of a hat, presumably to exclude surrounding light. Then he would put his face into the hat. It's kind of a strange image for us today...
> — Daniel Peterson, Prof. BYU, *Interview, PBS, The Mormons*

Unlike the Urim and Thummim which Joseph allegedly found buried along with the Gold Plates, Joseph found the Seer Stone while digging for a well.

> The seer stone referred to here was a chocolate-covered, somewhat egg-shaped stone which the Prophet found while digging a well in company with his brother Hyrum.
> — B. H. Roberts, LDS church historian, *Comprehensive History of the Church 1:129*

The evidence shows that the Urim and Thummim was an afterthought.

- Church records before 1833 do not mention the Urim and Thummim in connection with the translation of the Book of Mormon.
- The Book of Mormon is silent on the Urim and Thummim. However it does mention the seer stone.

> And the Lord said: I will prepare unto my servant Gazelem, a stone, which shall shine forth in darkness unto light...
> — *Alma 37:23*

- *Doctrine and Covenants* 10:1 was edited in 1835 to insert the Urim and Thummim.

1833 First Edition Book of Commandments, Chapter IX	1835 Second Edition Doctrine and Covenants, Section XXXVI
Now, behold I say unto you, that because you delivered up so many writings, which you had power to translate, into the hands of a wicked man, you have lost them, and you also lost your gift at the same time...	Now, behold I say unto you, that because you delivered up those writings which you had power given unto you to translate, by the means of the Urim and Thummim, into the hand of a wicked man, you have lost them; and you also lost your gift at the same time...

Conclusion

- Seer stones are associated with divination, something the Bible condemns. Lev. 19:26, Deut. 18:10, Jer. 14:14, Acts 16:16.
- The church manufactured the Urim and Thummim after-the-fact to divert attention as Joseph Smith was tried and convicted in New York for deceiving others that he could find buried treasure by looking at seer stones.

Lost 116 Pages

The first 116 pages of the original manuscript of the Book of Mormon were lost.

- Joseph Smith's mother recorded this event.

    > Martin Harris, having written some one hundred and sixteen pages for Joseph, asked permission of my son to carry the manuscript home with him, in order to let his wife read it, as he hoped it might have a salutary effect upon her feelings...
    >
    > After leaving Joseph he arrived at home with the manuscript in safety. Soon after he exhibited the manuscript to his wife...
    >
    > For a short time previous to Joseph's arrival, Mr. Harris had been otherwise engaged, and thought but little about the manuscript. When Joseph sent for him, he went immediately to the drawer where he had left it, but, behold it was gone! He asked his wife where it was. She solemnly averred that she did not know anything respecting it.
    > — Lucy Smith, Joseph Smith's mother, *Biographical Sketches, ch.25*

If Joseph Smith truly translated the gold plates then we would expect him to be able to reproduce a second nearly identical translation. This would be an opportunity to demonstrate that Joseph did indeed possess a supernatural gift.

However if Joseph was making the story up then we would not expect him to be able to reproduce it verbatim. Rehashing 116 pages from memory may recover major themes but he would not be able to recall every embellishing detail from his original creation.

Joseph's Response

Joseph needed to come up with a clever way to reproduce his narrative without all of the details lest he be exposed as a fraud. To solve this, Joseph claimed that God forbade him to produce a second translation as evidently whoever took the pages intended to alter the handwritten text!

- Lucy recorded Joseph's explanation.

    There is no doubt but Mrs. Harris took it from the drawer, with the view of retaining it, until another translation should be given, then, to alter the original translation, for the purpose of showing a discrepancy between them, and thus make the whole appear to be a deception.
    — Lucy Smith, Joseph Smith's mother, *Biographical Sketches, ch.25*

Conveniently Joseph claimed that the ancient authors had left a second less detailed record that coincidently covered the same period as the missing 116 pages. Joseph would translate from these, called *the Small Plates of Nephi*, and revert back to the more detailed large plates when caught up.

1830 Book of Mormon Preface

The original 1830 Book of Mormon contained this preface (removed in subsequent editions)

TO THE READER—

As many false reports have been circulated respecting the following work, and also many unlawful measures taken by the evil designing persons to destroy me, and also the work, I would inform you that I translated, by the gift and power of God, and caused to be written, one hundred and sixteen pages, the which I took from the Book of Lehi, which was an account abridged from the plates of Lehi, by the hand of Mormon; which said account, some person or persons have stolen and kept from me, notwithstanding my utmost exertions to recover it again—and being commanded of the Lord that I should not translate the same over again, for Satan had put it into their hearts to tempt the Lord their God, by altering the words, that they did read contrary from that which I translated and caused to be written; and if I should bring forth the same words again, or, in other words, if I should translate the same over again, they would publish that which they had stolen, and Satan would stir up the hearts of this generation, that they might not receive this work: but behold, the Lord said unto me, I will not suffer that Satan shall accomplish his evil design in this thing: therefore thou shalt translate from the plates of Nephi, until ye come to that which ye have translated, which ye have retained; and behold ye shall publish it as the record of Nephi; and thus I will confound those who have altered my words. I will not suffer that they shall destroy my work; yea, I will shew unto them that my wisdom is greater than the cunning of the Devil. Wherefore, to be obedient unto the commandments of God, I have, through his grace and mercy, accomplished that which he hath commanded me respecting this thing. I would also inform you that the plates of which hath been spoken, were found in the township of Manchester, Ontario county, New-York.

THE AUTHOR.

Conclusion

Joseph gambled that claiming to have a second set of plates would give him cover to produce a different text with the same themes but without the original detail. Only the ardent find this believable.

Archaeology

"The scientific study of historic or prehistoric peoples and their cultures by analysis of their artifacts, inscriptions, monuments, and other such remains, especially those that have been excavated."

— *Dictionary.com*

If the Book of Mormon is an authentic historical record of real people, languages, and cultures, then we would expect to find tangible evidences that corroborate it—unless of course it is a work of Joseph Smith's imagination.

The Archaeological Record

Comparing the Book of Mormon narrative with the Archaeological record.

Book of Mormon	Archaeology
People Nephites, Lamanites, Mulekites. Jews are the principle ancestors of the indigenous inhabitants.	Book of Mormon peoples are unknown. Analysis demonstrates indigenous inhabitants are of Asian descent. Evidence indicates extremely strong biological and cultural affinities between New World and Asian populations and leave no doubt that the first migrants into the Americas were Asians, possibly from Siberia. — Michael H. Crawford, Dept. of Anthropology, University of Kansas, *The Origins of Native Americans, p.3-4*
Geography *The Church of Jesus Christ of Latter-day Saints* offers no answer as to where the events in the Book of Mormon take place.	Because of this vacuum, Mormon apologists and members are left only to speculate, of which there is no consensus: • **Baja Peninsula** http://www.achoiceland.com/ • **Hemispheric** http://www.bookofmormongeography.net/ http://www.thebookofmormongeography.com/

	- **Great Lakes Region** http://www.bookofmormongeography.org/ http://www.bookofmormonevidence.org/ - **Central America/Mesoamerica** http://www.mormongeography.com/ http://bomgeography.poulsenll.org/ http://mormonmesoamerica.com/ - **New York** http://www.bookofmormonlands.com/ http://www.bookofmormonpromisedland.com/
Language *Reformed Egyptian* and possibly Hebrew.	The Book of Mormon suddenly appears with no other extant copies, fragments, quotations, citations, inscriptions, engravings, carvings, parchments, scrolls, etc. found. Hebrew and Egyptian have never been found in the ancient New World. Of all the peoples of the pre-Columbian New World, only the ancient Maya had a complete script. — Michael D. Coe, Prof. Yale University, *Breaking the Maya Code*, preface
Agriculture Wheat, Barley, Figs **Animals** Cattle, oxen, ass, horses, goats, sheep, swine, elephants **Coinage** *Alma 11.5-20* **Industry** Chariots, Compass, Windows **Metallurgy** Steel, Smelting, Dross **Weaponry** Chariots, Steel Swords, Archery, Scimitars **Religion** Judaism, Christianity, Synagogues	There are no archaeological evidences for any of these existing in pre-Columbian America.

New World Archaeological Funding (NWAF)

The NWAF is part of BYU. From inception it was financed by the church to perform archaeological research for Book of Mormon evidences throughout Mesoamerica. After 17 fruitless years, its founder, Thomas Ferguson, lost his testimony and declared:

> You can't set Book of Mormon geography down anywhere — because it is fictional and will never meet the requirements of the dirt-archaeology. I should say — what is in the ground will never confirm to what is in the book.
> — Thomas Stuart Ferguson, NWAF Founder, *Letter dated February 2, 1976*

Smithsonian Institute

> The Smithsonian Institute has never used the Book of Mormon in any way as a scientific guide. Smithsonian archaeologists see no direct connection between the archaeology of the New World and the subject matter of the book.
> — Smithsonian Institute, *Letter to Institute for Religious Research, September 28, 1997*

National Geographic

> [Joseph] Smith's narration is not generally taken as a scientific source for the history of the Americas. Archaeologists and other scholars have long probed the hemisphere's past, and the Society does not know of anything found so far that has substantiated the Book of Mormon.
> — National Geographic, *Letter to Institute for Religious Research, August 12, 1998*

Conclusion

The Book of Mormon is an unverified translation from non-existent records written in an unknown language by unknown people from an unknown land.

Book of Mormon locations

The following is a list of named places in the Book of Mormon. <u>None</u> have been independently identified as actually existing.

Aaron
Ablom
Agosh plains
Akish wilderness
Alma valley
Ammonihah
Amnihu hill
Amulon
Angola
Ani-Anti
Antionum
Antiparah
Mt. Antipas
Antum
Boaz
Bountiful city
Bountiful, land
* Bountiful
City by the Sea
Comnor hill
Corihor, land
Corihor valley
Cumeni
* Cumorah hill
Land of David
Desolation, city
Desolation, land
Ephraim hill
Land of First Inheritance
Gad
Gadiandi
Gadiomnah
Gid
Gideon, city
Gideon, land
Gideon, valley
Gilgal, city
Gilgal, valley
Gimgimno
Hagoth
Helam
Hermounts
Heshlon
Heth
Irreantum
Ishmael
Jacob
Jacobugath
Jashon, city
Jashon, land
Jershon
Jerusalem
Jordan, city
Josh
Joshua
Judea
Kishkumen
Laman, city
Laman river
Lehi, city
Lehi, land of
Morianton
Lehi, land (south)
Lehi-Nephi, land
Lehi-Nephi, city
Lemuel, city
Lemuel, land
Manti, city
Manti, hill
Manti, land
Melek
Michmash
Middoni
Midian
Minon
Mocum
Moriancumer
Morianton, city
Morianton, land
Morianton, Nephite area
Mormon, forest
Mormon (region near city of Lehi-Nephi)
Mormon, waters
Moron
Moroni's camp
Moroni, land
Moroni, city
Moronihah
Mulek
* Nahom
Narrow Neck
Narrow Pass
Narrow Strip of Wilderness
Nehor
Nephi, city
Nephi, land
Nephihah, city
Nephihah, plains
Nephite Refuge
Noah, city
Noah, land
Ogath
Omner
Onidah
Onidah, hill
Onihah
Ramah hill
Riplah hill
Ripliancum, waters
Sebus, waters
Shazer
Shem, city
Shem, land
Shemlon
Sherrizah
Shilom, city
Shilom, land
Shim hill
Shimnilom
Shurr valley
Sidom
Sidon river
Siron
Teancum
Zarahemla, city
Zarahemla, land
Zeezrom
Zerin, mountain

* Some Mormon apologists claim to identify these locations

Conclusion

The Book of Mormon is either fact or fiction.

Fiction	?	Fact
Middle Earth J.R.R. Tolkien's *Lord of the Rings* names at least 279 locations. None to date have been independently identified because it is a work of fiction.	**Book of Mormon** Joseph Smith's *Book of Mormon* names at least 127 locations. None to date have been independently identified.	**The Bible** The 66 books of the biblical canon names over 1,200 locations, with hundreds independently identified. Visit http://www.OpenBible.info for Google Earth KMZ's, coordinates, and over 10,000 photos.

Bountiful

The Book of Mormon narrative follows a group of Jews who left Jerusalem for the New World in 600 B.C. Along the way they stopped at a tropical paradise somewhere on the Arabian peninsula. They called it "Bountiful" for its abundant fruit. This location is said to have also provided them with wild game, honey, ore, timber and resources to construct tools and a ship that would take them east across the Indian and Pacific oceans to the New World.

No proposed locations are recognized by the Mormon church.

While some Mormon apologists claim to have identified Bountiful, it's important to keep in mind that:

- *The Church of Jesus Christ of Latter-day Saints* has not endorsed any proposed location. Until then, claims made by apologists remain personal opinion and speculative.
- Much of the on-the-ground research by Mormon apologists have been conducted by amateurs.
- No non-Mormon researchers have independently confirmed the location of Bountiful.

Southern Dhofar

Some apologists have proposed the southern Dhofar region of Oman and Yemen to be the possible location for Bountiful, in particular Salalah, Khor Rori and Khor Kharfot.

- There is no consensus for a specific location among those who advocate a southern Dhofar location.
- It is debated that the area supports suitable tree growth to construct a durable transoceanic vessel.

> Aston feels that the larger species of trees indigenous to the Coastal Plain and Escarpment Mountains zones of Dhofar would have provided adequate timber for ship building, or perhaps as he suggests, raft building. I am not as convinced of this conclusion as is Aston...
>
> The largest tree[s] of Dhofar... all produce a wood that is too soft, heavy, and porous to withstand the rigors of a transoceanic crossing...
>
> Aston also suggests that his contemporary photos of "tall native hardwood trees" growing in Khor Kharfot lend support to his conclusion that the area is the most likely candidate for the site of the ship construction. I would suggest caution in accepting this conclusion for two reasons. First, the adjectives tall, native, and hardwood are rather subjective and in many cases questionable. I personally would not use such terms to describe the trees now growing in the area, and honestly would be very nervous about trusting my life to any watercraft constructed solely of such wood for a transoceanic crossing.
> — Terry Ball, archaeobotanist, Prof. BYU, *Journal of the Book of Mormon, Vol. 18, Iss. 1, p.56-57*

According to the Book of Mormon narrative, the location of Bountiful is inextricably linked to being nearly eastward from Nahom, of which location itself is unknown.

> And it came to pass that Ishmael died and was buried in the place which was called Nahom... and we did travel nearly eastward from that time forth.
> — *1 Nephi 16:34; 17:1*

Photographs provided by apologists are typically taken during the region's monsoon season (late June to October) which of course causes the dry vegetation to green.
Visit http://www.mormonhandbook.com/home/bountiful.html to see full color photo examples.

Contemporary photos may not accurately reflect the vegetation at the time of Nephi at Khor Kharfot or at other potential sites for Nephi's Bountiful.
— Terry B. Ball, Prof. BYU, archaeobotanist, *Journal of the Book of Mormon, Vol. 18, Iss. 1, p.56-57*

Conclusion

The evidences are insufficient and inconclusive to place Bountiful with any certainty to any of the proposed locations in the southern Dhofar region. Furthermore, that the LDS church today will not endorsed any Book of Mormon location is telling.

Hill Cumorah

The Book of Mormon narrative tells of two epic battles that took place on a hill named Cumorah.

- The first battle took place among the Jaredits, who called the hill Ramah (Ether 5:11)
- In the second battle the Lamanites destroy the Nephites (Mormon 6)
- The historical records of these people were buried in this same hill. (Mormon 6:6)
    - According to Joseph Smith, he found these records buried in a hill in Manchester, New York, a few miles from his home.

> Convenient to the village of Manchester, Ontario county, New York, stands a hill of considerable size, and the most elevated of any in the neighborhood. On the west side of this hill, not far from the top, under a stone of considerable size, lay the plates, deposited in a stone box.
>
> — Joseph Smith, Mormonism founder, *Testimony of Joseph Smith*

- Since 1829 this hill in New York has been called the Hill Cumorah.
- Joseph's translation of these alleged records is published as the Book of Mormon.

No Archaeological Evidence

If the Book of Mormon narrative were true, then this hill where these two epic battles were fought should be an archaeological gold mine. However the LDS church has not permitted any formal research or excavation there. Rather it constructed a visitor's center and holds an annual pageant there.

Hill Cumorah Statements

That the Book of Mormon's Hill Cumorah is in New York poses a problem for some modern Mormon apologists who deem that Central America and its ancient ruins are a better fit for Book of Mormon geography than New York. Those who advocate this position are at odds with General Authorities.

> The Church has long maintained, as attested to by references in the writings of General Authorities, that the Hill Cumorah in western New York state is the same as referenced in the Book of Mormon.
> — F. Michael Watson, First Presidency Secretary, *Letter dated October 16, 1990*

> It is known that the Hill Cumorah where the Nephites were destroyed is the hill where the Jaredites were also destroyed. This hill was known to the Jaredites as Rama...
>
> The Prophet Joseph Smith himself is on record, definitely declaring the present hill called Cumorah to be the exact hill spoken of in the Book of Mormon.
>
> Further, the fact that all of his associates from the beginning down have spoken of it as the identical hill where Mormon and Moroni hid the records, must carry some weight. It is difficult for a reasonable person to believe that such men as Oliver Cowdery, Brigham Young, Parley P. Pratt, Orson Pratt, David Whitmer, and many others, could speak frequently of the Spot where the Prophet Joseph Smith obtained the plates as the Hill Cumorah, and not be corrected by the Prophet, if that were not the fact. That they did speak of this hill in the days of the Prophet in this definite manner is an established record of history..."
> — Joseph Fielding Smith, Mormon prophet, *Doctrines of Salvation, Vol.3, p.232-43*

> In the western part of the state of New York near Palmyra is a prominent hill known as the "hill Cumorah." (Morm. 6:6.) On July twenty-fifth of this year, as I stood on the crest of that hill admiring with awe the breathtaking panorama which stretched out before me

on every hand, my mind reverted to the events which occurred in that vicinity some twenty-five centuries ago—events which brought to an end the great Jaredite nation...

This second civilization to which I refer, the Nephites, flourished in America between 600 B.C. and A.D. 400. Their civilization came to an end for the same reason, at the same place, and in the same manner as did the Jaredites'.
— Marion G. Romney, First Presidency Counselor, *Ensign, November 1975, p.35*

Both the Nephite and Jaredite civilizations fought their final great wars of extinction at and near the Hill Cumorah (or Ramah as the Jaredites termed it), which hill is located between Palmyra and Manchester in the western part of the State of New York.

Joseph Smith, Oliver Cowdery and many of the early brethren, who were familiar with all the circumstances attending the coming forth of the Book of Mormon in this dispensation, have left us a pointed testimony as to the identity and location of Cumorah or Ramah.
— Bruce R. McConkie, Mormon apostle, *Mormon Doctrine, p. 174-175*

This time it will have to do with so important a matter as a war of extinction of two peoples, the Nephites and the Jaredites, on the self same battle site, with the same 'hill' marking the axis of military movements. By the Nephites this 'hill' was called the 'Hill Cumorah,' by the Jaredites the 'Hill Ramah'; it was that same 'hill,' in which the Nephite records were deposited by Mormon and Moroni, and from which Joseph Smith obtained the Book of Mormon, therefore the 'Mormon Hill,' of today—since the coming forth of the Book of Mormon—near Palmyra, New York.
— B. H. Roberts, LDS church historian, *Studies of the Book of Mormon, p.277*

The hill, which was known by one division of the ancient peoples as Cumorah, by another as Ramah, is situated near Palmyra in the State of New York.
— James E. Talmage, Mormon apostle, *Articles of Faith, Lecture 14, p.262*

The great and last battle, in which several hundred thousand Nephites perished was on the hill Cumorah, the same hill from which the plates were taken by Joseph Smith.
— Orson Pratt, Mormon apostle, *Journal of Discourses 14:331*

Finally, they became so utterly wicked, so fully ripened for destruction, that one branch of the nation, called the Nephites, gathered their entire people around the hill Cumorah, in the State of New York, in Ontario County; and the Lamanites, the opposite army, gathered by millions in the same region.
— Orson Pratt, Mormon apostle, *Journal of Discourses 17:30*

Thirty-six years prior to this time his nation was destroyed in what we term the State of New York, around about a hill, called by that people the Hill of Cumorah, when many hundreds of thousands of the Nephites—men, women and children, fell, during the greatest battle that they had had with the Lamanites.
— Orson Pratt, Mormon apostle, *Journal of Discourses 20:63*

Cumorah, the artificial hill of north America, is well calculated to stand in this generation, as a monument of marvelous works and wonders. Around that mount died millions of the Jaredites; yea, there ended one of the greatest nations of this earth. In that day, her inhabitants spread from sea to sea, and enjoyed national greatness and glory, nearly fifteen hundred years.
That people forsook the Lord and died in wickedness. There, too, fell the Nephites, after they had forgotten the Lord that bought them.
— *Messenger and Advocate, Vol. 2, No. 2, p.220*

I must now give you some description of the place where, and the manner in which these records were deposited...

You are acquainted with the mail road from Palmyra, Wayne Co. to Canandaigua, Ontario Co. N. Y. and also, as you pass from the former to the latter place, before arriving at the little village of Manchester, say from three to four, or about four miles from Palmyra, you pass a large hill on the east side of the road...

between these hills, the entire power and national strength of both the Jaredites and Nephites were destroyed.

— Oliver Cowdery, Assistant President and Book of Mormon witness, *Messenger and Advocate Vol. 1, No.1, p.158*

Conclusion

With the absence of archaeological evidence casting a large shadow of doubt over the authenticity of Book of Mormon, that the church has not excavated this hill is telling. The rational must be that it is better to be left wondering what is in the dirt than to know for certain and be disappointed.

Nahom

The Book of Mormon narrative follows a group of Jews that left Jerusalem for the New World in 600 B.C. Along the way they stopped at a place called Nahom.

From Jerusalem to Nahom

The narrative suggests that after they left Jerusalem they traveled:

- Down the Arabian Peninsula paralleling the Red Sea in a "nearly south-southeast direction" (1 Nephi 16:13)
- Until they arrived at "the place called Nahom" (1 Nephi 16:34)
- From there they turned and traveled in a "nearly eastward" direction (1 Nephi 17:1)
- Crossed the Arabian Desert, in particular the uninhabited Rub' al Khali (aka "Empty Quarter"), the world's largest sand sea.
- And arrived at a tropical paradise, somewhere on the east coast of the peninsula, and named it Bountiful for its abundant fruit.

No proposed locations are recognized by the LDS church

While some Mormon apologists claim to have identified Bountiful, it's important to keep in mind that:

- *The Church of Jesus Christ of Latter-day Saints* has not endorsed any proposed location. Until then, claims made by apologists remain personal opinion and speculative.
- Much of the on-the-ground research provided by Mormon apologists have been conducted by amateurs.
- No non-Mormon researchers have independently confirmed the location of Nahom.

Nahom = Nihm?

Some Mormon apologists see a link between Nahom and the name of the Nihm tribe in Yemen. The Nihm tribe today is located about 25 miles north of Sana'a, Yemen. An altar inscription dated to the 7th-6th century B.C. reads "son of Naw'an the Nihmite", which may be evidence that the tribe dates back to 600 B.C.

- This link is made on the basis that Semitic languages do not use vowels, therefore the consonant spelling of Nahom (NHM) can be compared to Nihm (NHM).
- But a linguistic link is an assumption.

> The exact equivalency of the root letters cannot be assured. It is probable that the term Nahom was spelled with the rasped or fricative Hebrew letter for "h" (het or chet) whereas the name Nihm, both in modern Arabic and in the ancient Sabaean dialect, is spelled with a softer, less audible h sound... One has to assume, it seems to me, that when the members of Lehi's party heard the local name for "the place that was called Nahom" they associated the sound of that local name with the term Nahom, a Hebrew word that was familiar to and had meaning for them.
> — S. Kent Brown, director of the BYU Jerusalem Center, *Journal of Book of Mormon Studies: Vol.8, Iss.1, pp.66-68*

- A linguistic link to a Hebrew word is also an assumption, as the Book of Mormon was allegedly written in reformed Egyptian, which is an unknown language.
- The name of a *tribe* does not necessarily give us the name of a *place*.
- According to the Book of Mormon narrative, the location of Nahom is inextricably linked to being nearly westward of Bountiful, of which location itself is unknown.

Seven Years In The Desert

The photo at left is the Arabian Desert as delineated by the WWFN. The Empty Quarter, considered impassable, encompasses the bottom third of the peninsula and is the largest sand sea in the world.

It is highly likely that a group of Jews traveling down the Arabian peninsula would have followed the ancient Frankincense Trail. It would have been suicide to abandon the trail's watering holes to cut east across the uninhabited Empty Quarter.

- The narrative says that it took them eight years to reach Bountiful from Jerusalem (1 Nephi 17:4)
- A Mormon apologist places the time it took them to reach Nahom at about a year.

> I believe that it took them about a year to go from their first base camp down to Nahom. The reason is because that's when Nephi mentions the birth of the first children.
> — S. Kent Brown, director of the BYU Jerusalem Center, *Journey of Faith DVD*

- If it took one year to reach Nahom, that means it took them seven years to reach Bountiful. That's seven years crossing the Empty Quarter. Apologists acknowledge how daunting travel through this desert is.

> They're going in an area that no one is his right mind would have gone. This space in the Arabian desert—out in a wilderness where you can barely survive four or five hours without water.
> — Thomas G. Madsen, *Journey of Faith DVD*

Moving the turn *nearly eastward* farther south

To mitigate the absurdity that a group of Jews survived seven years crossing the Empty Quarter, apologists have been moving the spot where the Jews would have turned to head towards Bountiful to get it below the Empty Quarter.

- The earliest model, proposed by Hugh Nibley, has the turn around the 19th parallel.
- The most recent model, proposed by S. Kent Brown, has the turn around the 14th parallel.

Evolving Models

Nibley (1950)

Sources: Nibley, Lehi in the Desert, Improvement Era, 1950

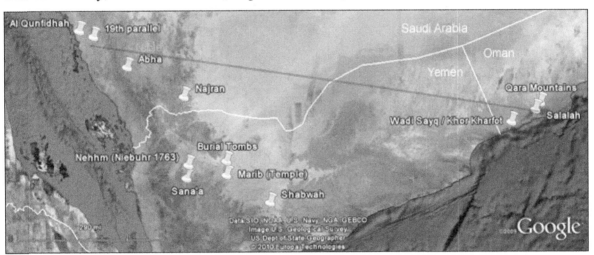

The late Hugh Nibley, a professor at BYU, and considered the foremost Mormon apologist of his day, offered one of the earliest models linking Nahom to Bountiful.

- Proposes the Qara Mountains in the southern region of Dhofar as the possible site of Bountiful.
- Proposes the turn to Bountiful near 19th parallel.

Hilton (1976)

Sources: Hilton & Hilton, Ensign, Sep. 1976, p.33, Oct. 1976, pp.34-35

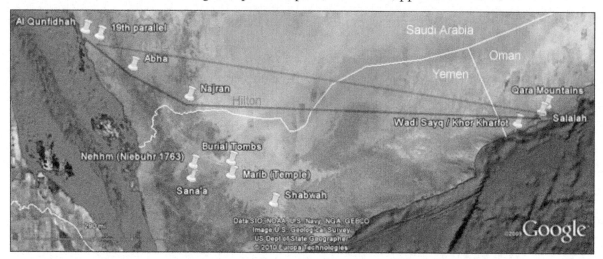

Amateurs Lynn and Hope Hilton, a married couple, were approached by the Ensign, a church periodical, to photograph and investigate Nibley's model.

- Proposes Al Qunfidhah, Saudi Arabia, a coastal village which sits along the Red Sea near the 19th parallel as the possible site of Nahom.

- Proposes that the Jews continued traveling south-southeast through Abha to Najral, Saudi Arabia, before turning east toward Bountiful.

- Proposes Salalah, Oman, which sits at the base of the Qara Mountains, as the location of Bountiful.

- Proposes that the Jews would not have crossed into Yemen to avoid the Sabaean kingdom. All later models ignore this concern.

Christensen (1978)

Sources: Christensen, Ensign, Aug. 1978, p.73

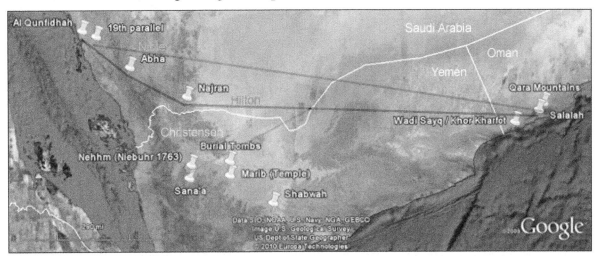

Ross T. Christensen, a BYU professor of archaeology and anthropology, found a 1763 Carsten Niebuhr map which labeled an area "Nehhm" about 25 miles north of Sana'a, Yemen. This location generally corresponds to the present location of the Nihm tribe today.

- Proposes that Lehi's route dipped down into Yemen to this general area and then reverted back up to meet the Hilton route.

Aston (1986)

Sources: Aston & Aston, Lehi's Trail and Nahom Revisited, Maxwell Institute; Journal of Book of Mormon Studies, Vol.7, Iss.1, pp.4-11

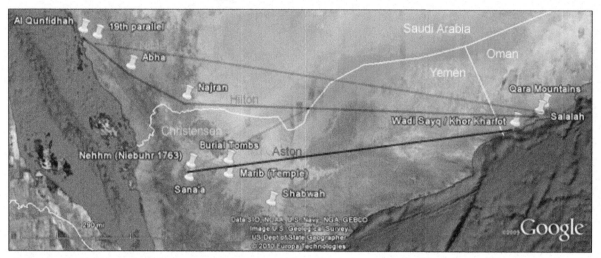

Amateurs Warren and Michaela Aston, a married couple from Australia, were intrigued by Christensen's model and visited Yemen.

- Found a map at the University of Sana'a, Yemen, that corroborated Nieburh's "Nehhm".
- Proposes Khor Kharfot, about 40 miles down the coast from Salalah, as an alternative location for Bountiful.

Brown (2003)

Sources: Brown, Journal of Book of Mormon Studies, Vol.8, Iss.1, pp.66-68; Vol.12, Iss.1, pp.111-12, Journey of Faith DVD

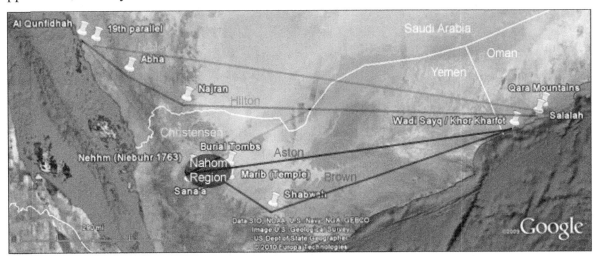

Scott Kent Brown is the director of the BYU Jerusalem Center.

- Proposes that "Nahom" is a large region, possibly encompassing:
    - Marib, Yemen, about 73 miles southeast of the current Nihm tribal area, where the altar inscriptions were found.
    - Ancient burial tombs located about 25 miles north of Marib, which he suggests may be supporting evidence of Ishmael's burial (1 Nephi 16:34).
- Proposes that the nearly eastward direction to Bountiful is not the route traveled, but rather the location of Bountiful in relation to Nahom.
- Proposes that the Jews traveled as far south as Shabwah, Yemen, before turning east towards Bountiful. While this model keeps the Jews on the outskirts of the Empty Quarter, it doesn't fit the narrative that from Nahom they traveled nearly eastward from that time forth to Bountiful.

Conclusion

The evidences are insufficient to place Nahom with any certainty to any of the proposed locations. There just isn't much to work with here.

- One verse in the Book of Mormon that mentions "a place called Nahom"
- A modern Yemeni tribe called Nihm
- A 7th-6th century B.C. altar inscription that reads "son of Naw'an the Nihmite"

To make this fit apologists have to make several assumptions:

- A linguistic assumption that Joseph's English *Nahom*, which he allegedly translated from an unknown reformed Egyptian language, is connected to the Nihm tribe in Yemen.
- An assumption that there was a place in 600 B.C. named after the Nihm tribe.
- An assumption that a group of Jews that had lived in Jerusalem all of their lives could survive seven years crossing the Empty Quarter.

That the LDS church will not endorsed this Book of Mormon location is telling.

Book of Mormon Authorship

Does the Book of Mormon exhibit evidence of divine/ancient origins or human/modern origins?

5,000 Changes

Despite the claim that Joseph Smith's "translation" was by the gift and power of God, several thousand changes have been made to the Book of Mormon since its original printing.

Absurdities

The Book of Mormon narrative is full of absurdities that demonstrate its a work of fiction.

King James style

Despite the Book of Mormon being published in 1830, its narrative attempts to employ the antiquated English style of the Early Modern Era, as though to make it read more like the King James Version of the Bible published in 1611.

Wordiness

Joseph Smith claimed that the Book of Mormon was his translation of an ancient book written upon gold plates. Its long-windedness is contrary to what we would expect given the size of the plates.

Anachronisms

Animals and objects that appear throughout the Book of Mormon story confirm its 19th century origins, not the ancient history it purports to be.

Plagiarism

Earlier works, like Ethan Smith's *View of the Hebrews*, provide a working framework for the Book of Mormon's themes. Joseph also borrows extensively from the Bible.

Isaiah

The extensive quoting from the King James translation of Isaiah poses several problems for the Book of Mormon to be considered an authentic ancient record.

Did Joseph Smith author the Book of Mormon?

- According to Joseph's mother, Lucy Smith, he possessed a vivid imagination and was telling stories with Book of Mormon themes years before he allegedly found the gold plates.

> During our evening conversations, Joseph would occasionally give us some of the most amusing recitals that could be imagined. He would describe the ancient inhabitants of this continent, their dress, mode of traveling, and the animals upon which they rode; their cities, their buildings, with every particular; their mode of warfare; and also their religious worship. This he would do with as much ease, seemingly, as if he had spent his whole life with them.
> — Lucy Smith, *Biographical Sketches, p.345*

- LDS historian B. H. Roberts shares Lucy's view.

> That such power of imagination would have to be of a high order is conceded; that Joseph Smith possessed such a gift of mind there can be no question.
> — B.H. Roberts, Mormon Seventy and LDS church historian, *Studies of the Book of Mormon, p.243*

- Joseph was listed as the Author and Proprietor in the first edition of the Book of Mormon. This was changed to Translator in subsequent editions.

- Joseph intended to sell the Book of Mormon copyright:

Joseph looked into the hat in which he placed the stone, and received a revelation that some of the brethren should go to Toronto, Canada, and that they would sell the copyright of the Book of Mormon.
— David Whitmer, Mormon apostle and Book of Mormon witnesses, *An Address to all Believers in Christ, p.31*

Conclusion

The evidence leads to one conclusion: Joseph Smith had the materials and the imagination to create the Book of Mormon story.

5,000 Changes to the Book of Mormon

"I told the brethren that the Book of Mormon was the most correct of any book on earth, and the keystone of our religion, and a man would get nearer to God by abiding by its precepts, than by any other book."
— *Joseph Smith*

Since its first publication in 1830, the Book of Moron has undergone thousands of changes.

- In *The Book of Mormon, The Earliest Text*, Royal Skousen, a professor of linguistics at BYU and a recognized expert of the textual history of the Book of Mormon, identified 5,280 variations in all editions of the Book of Mormon.
- In *3,913 Changes in the Book of Mormon*, Jerald and Sandra Tanner identified nearly 4,000 changes when comparing the original 1830 edition to the 1964 edition.

Doctrinal Changes
A selection of doctrinal changes in the Book of Mormon.

Godhead
Changes were made to the Book of Mormon after Joseph Smith changed his doctrine from Monotheism to Polytheism.

	1830 original edition	**1837 and subsequent editions**
1 Nephi 11:18	And he said unto me: Behold, the virgin which thou seest is the mother of God after the manner of the flesh.	And he said unto me: Behold, the virgin whom thou seest is the mother of <u>the Son of</u> God, after the manner of the flesh.
1 Nephi 11:21	And the angel said unto me: Behold the Lamb of God, yea, even the Eternal Father.	And the angel said unto me: Behold the Lamb of God, yea, even <u>the Son of</u> the Eternal Father!

1 Nephi 11:32	...And I looked and beheld the Lamb of God, that he was taken by the people, yea, the everlasting God was judged of the world.	...And I looked and beheld the Lamb of God, that he was taken by the people; yea, <u>the Son of</u> the everlasting God was judged of the world.
1 Nephi 13:40	...that the Lamb of God is the Eternal Father and the Savior of the world...	...that the Lamb of God is <u>the Son of</u> the Eternal Father, and the Savior of the world...

Racism

The church made changes to the Book of Mormon to soften its racism.

	1830 original edition	**1981 edition**
2 Nephi 30:6	And then shall they rejoice; for they shall know that it is a blessing unto them from the hand of God; and their scales of darkness shall begin to fall from their eyes; and many generations shall not pass away among them, save they shall be a <u>white</u> and a delightsome people.	And then shall they rejoice; for they shall know that it is a blessing unto them from the hand of God; and their scales of darkness shall begin to fall from their eyes; and many generations shall not pass away among them, save they shall be a ~~white~~ <u>pure</u> and a delightsome people.

And changes to chapter headings:

	1981 edition	**2010 online edition**
2 Nephi, ch. 5	The Nephites separate themselves from the Lamanites, keep the law of Moses, and build a temple—Because of their unbelief, the Lamanites are cursed, <u>receive a skin of blackness</u>, and become a scourge unto the Nephites.	The Nephites separate themselves from the Lamanites, keep the law of Moses, and build a temple—Because of their unbelief, the Lamanites are cursed, ~~receive a skin of blackness~~ <u>cut off from the presence of the Lord</u>, are cursed, and become a scourge unto the Nephites.

Mormon, ch. 5	Mormon again leads the Nephite armies in battles of blood and carnage—The Book of Mormon shall come forth to convince all Israel that Jesus is the Christ—<u>The Lamanites shall be a dark, filthy, and loathsome people</u>—They shall receive the gospel from the Gentiles in the latter days.	Mormon again leads the Nephite armies in battles of blood and carnage—The Book of Mormon will come forth to convince all Israel that Jesus is the Christ—~~The Lamanites shall be a dark, filthy, and loathsome people~~ <u>Because of their unbelief, the Lamanites will be scattered, and the Spirit will cease to strive with them</u>—They will receive the gospel from the Gentiles in the latter days.

Alterable Decrees

The evolving doctrines of the church necessitated editing the Book of Mormon's teaching that God's decrees are unalterable.

	1830 original edition	**1837 edition until 1981**
Alma 29:4	I ought not to harrow up in my desires the firm decree of a just God, for I know that he granteth unto men according to their desire, whether it be unto death or unto life; yea, I know that he allotteth unto men, <u>yea, decreeth unto them decrees which are unalterable</u>, according to their wills, whether they be unto salvation or unto destruction.	I ought not to harrow up in my desires the firm decree of a just God, for I know that he granteth unto men according to their desire, whether it be unto death or unto life; yea, I know that he allotteth unto men, ~~yea, decreeth unto them decrees which are unalterable~~, according to their wills, whether they be unto salvation or unto destruction.

Correcting Errors

A selection of errors in the Book of Mormon.

Christ named too soon

The name of Christ is not revealed until 2 Nephi 10:3.

> Wherefore, as I said unto you, it must needs be expedient that Christ—for in the last night the angel spake unto me that this should be his name.
>
> — *2 Nephi 10:3*

So "Jesus Christ" had to be replaced with "the Messiah" in 1 Nephi 12:18.

	1830 original edition	**1837 and subsequent editions**
1 Nephi 12:18	Yea, even the word of the justice of the Eternal God, <u>and Jesus Christ</u> who is the Lamb of God.	Yea, even the word of the justice of the Eternal God, ~~and Jesus Christ~~ <u>the Messiah</u> who is the Lamb of God.

King Benjamin alive after being dead

Mosiah 6:5 records king Benjamin's death. Later in the narrative the author forgot that king Benjamin had died, which necessitated replacing him with another king.

	1830 original edition	**1837 and subsequent editions**
Mosiah 21:28	...king <u>Benjamin</u> had a gift from God.	...king ~~Benjamin~~ <u>Mosiah</u> had a gift from God.
Ether 4:1	...and for this cause did king <u>Benjamin</u> keep them...	...and for this cause did king ~~Benjamin~~ <u>Mosiah</u> keep them...

From Author to Translator

The original 1830 edition named Joseph Smith as "Author and Proprietor". After Joseph could not sell the Book of Mormon copyright, all subsequent editions named him "Translator".

More changes

A selection of various changes from the many thousands in the Book of Mormon

	1830 first edition	**1840 and subsequent editions**
1 Nephi 20:1	...and are come forth out of the waters of Judah, which swear by the name of the Lord...	...and are come forth out of the waters of Judah, <u>or out of the waters of baptism</u>, who swear by the name of the Lord...

	1830 original edition	**1981 edition**
Alma 32:30	But behold, as the seed swelleth, and sprouteth, and beginneth to grow, then you must needs say that the seed is good; for behold it swelleth, and sprouteth, and beginneth to grow.	But behold, as the seed swelleth, and sprouteth, and beginneth to grow, then you must needs say that the seed is good; for behold it swelleth, and sprouteth, and beginneth to grow. <u>And now, behold, will not this strengthen your faith? Yea, it will strengthen your faith: for ye will say I know that this is a good seed; for behold it sprouteth and beginneth to grow.</u>

	1830 original edition	**1837 edition until 1981**
3 Nephi 3:23	And the land which was appointed was the land of Zarahemla, <u>and the land which was between the land Zarahemla</u> and the land Bountiful, yea, to the line which was between the land Bountiful and the land Desolation.	And the land which was appointed was the land of Zarahemla, ~~and the land which was between the land Zarahemla~~ and the land Bountiful, yea, to the line which was between the land Bountiful and the land Desolation.

	1830 original edition	**1837 and subsequent editions**
3 Nephi 10:4	O ye people of these great cities which have fallen, which are the descendant of Jacob; yea, which are of the house of Israel; <u>O ye people of the house of Israel,</u> how oft have I gathered you as a hen gathereth her chickens under her wings, and have nourished you.	O ye people of these great cities which have fallen, who are descendants of Jacob, yea, who are of the house of Israel, ~~O ye people of the house of Israel~~ how oft have I gathered you as a hen gathereth her chickens under her wings, and have nourished you.

	1830 original edition	**1837 edition until 1981**
3 Nephi 16:10	...and if they shall do all those things, <u>and shall reject the fulness of my gospel</u>, behold, saith the Father, I will bring the fulness of my gospel from among them.	...and if they shall do all those things, ~~and shall reject the fulness of my gospel~~, behold, saith the Father, I will bring the fulness of my gospel from among them.

	1830 original edition	**1837 edition until 1981**
Mormon 9:34	But the Lord knoweth the things which we have written, and also that none other people knoweth our language; <u>and because that none other people knoweth our language</u>, therefore he hath prepared means for the interpretation thereof.	But the Lord knoweth the things which we have written, and also that none other people knoweth our language; ~~and because that none other people knoweth our language~~, therefore he hath prepared means for the interpretation thereof.

Conclusion

The thousands of changes throughout the editions of the Book of Mormon raise serious doubts about Joseph Smith's claim that his translation of the Book of Mormon was by the gift and power of God.

Absurdities in the Book of Mormon

Egyptian Language

The author of the Book of Mormon evidently didn't realize that Jews would not speak or write in the language of Egypt, a nation that enslaved them and that the Jews despised.

> Yea, I make a record in the language of my father, which consists of the learning of the Jews and the language of the Egyptians.
> — *1 Nephi 1:2*

> For it were not possible that our father, Lehi, could have remembered all these things, to have taught them to his children, except it were for the help of these plates; for he having been taught in the language of the Egyptians therefore he could read these engravings, and teach them to his children, that thereby they could teach them to their children, and so fulfilling the commandments of God, even down to this present time.
> — *Mosiah 1:4*

> And now, behold, we have written this record according to our knowledge, in the characters which are called among us the reformed Egyptian, being handed down and altered by us, according to our manner of speech.
> — *Mormon 9:32*

Submarines

Around 2,500 B.C. in the Book of Mormon narrative the Jaredites built submarines.

> For behold, ye shall be as a whale in the midst of the sea; for the mountain waves shall dash upon you.
> — *Ether 2:24*

> And it came to pass that when they were buried in the deep there was no water that could hurt them, their vessels being tight like unto a dish.
> *— Ether 6:7*

> And thus they were driven forth; and no monster of the sea could break them, neither whale that could mar them; and they did have light continually, whether it was above the water or under the water.
> *— Ether 6:10*

- A submersible watertight vessel needs an oxygen source. The solution: plugs on the top and the bottom!

> And also we shall perish, for in them we cannot breathe, save it is the air which is in them; therefore we shall perish. And the Lord said unto the brother of Jared: Behold, thou shalt make a hole in the top, and also in the bottom; and when thou shalt suffer for air thou shalt unstop the hole and receive air. And if it be so that the water come in upon thee, behold, ye shall stop the hole, that ye may not perish in the flood.
> *— Ether 2:19-20*

Shiz

It evidently didn't dawn on the author of the Book of Mormon that a decapitated man would not be struggling for breath after-the-fact.

> And it came to pass that when Coriantumr had leaned upon his sword, that he rested a little, he smote off the head of Shiz. And it came to pass that after he had smitten off the head of Shiz, that Shiz raised up on his hands and fell; and after that he had struggled for breath, he died.
> *— Ether 15:30-31*

The Babylon Exile

The Book of Mormon narrative opens with a prophet named Lehi who warns the city of Jerusalem to repent lest the city be destroyed and its peoples taken captive to Babylon. In response the people mock at him.

> ...There came many prophets, prophesying unto the people that they must repent, or the great city Jerusalem must be destroyed... and the inhabitants thereof; many should perish by the sword, and many should be carried away captive into Babylon... And it came to pass that the Jews did mock him... they were angry with him.
> — *1 Nephi 1:4,13,19-20*

- The Book of Mormon dates this event to the "first year of the reign of Zedekiah" (1 Nephi 1:4).
- The author of the Book of Mormon was evidently unaware that the Babylonians had already sieged Jerusalem and exiled its people.
- The first Babylonian siege and exile happened under king Jehoiachin (2 Kings 24:13).
- All Jerusalem was taken captive except the poor (2 Kings 24:14).
- Jehoiachin served only three months (2 Kings 24:8) before the Babylonian king Nebuchadnezzar appointed his uncle Zedekiah as king (2 Kings 24:17).
- According to the Book of Mormon, Lehi's warnings to Jerusalem happened in the first year of Zedekiah's reign, *after* the deportation.
    - The Book of Mormon narrative is oblivious that an exile had already taken place.
    - We would not expect those left behind in Jerusalem to mock that which they had already witnessed was possible.
    - According to the Book of Mormon narrative, Lehi, a lifetime citizen of Jerusalem (1 Nephi 1:4) wasn't poor so he should have been taken captive with Jehoiachin.

> And it came to pass that he departed into the wilderness. And he left his house, and the land of his inheritance, and his gold, and his silver, and his precious things, and took nothing with him...
> — *1 Nephi 2:4*

Solomon's Temple Replica

Construction of Solomon's Temple was a major undertaking.

- 30,000 laborers (1 Kings 5:13)
- 70,000 transporters (1 Kings 5:15)
- 80,000 stone hewers (1 Kings 5:15)
- 3,300 deputies (1 Kings 5:16)
- Construction took seven years (1 Kings 6:38)

According to the Book of Mormon narrative, the Jews who settled in the New World constructed a replica of Solomon's Temple.

> And I, Nephi, did build a temple; and I did construct it after the manner of the temple of Solomon save it were not built of so many precious things; for they were not to be found upon the land, wherefore, it could not be built like unto Solomon's temple. But the manner of the construction was like unto the temple of Solomon; and the workmanship thereof was exceedingly fine.
> — *2 Nephi 5:16*

The prior verse contradicts the claim "so many precious things were not to be found on the land"

> And I did teach my people to build buildings, and to work in all manner of <u>wood</u>, and of <u>iron</u>, and of copper, and of <u>brass</u>, and of steel, and of <u>gold</u>, and of <u>silver</u>, and of precious ores, <u>which were in great abundance</u>.
> — *2 Nephi 5:15*

This list in nearly identical to the materials used to construct Solomon's Temple.

> Now send me a skilled man to work in <u>gold</u>, <u>silver</u>, <u>brass</u> and <u>iron</u>, and in purple, crimson and violet fabrics...to prepare <u>timber</u> in abundance for me, for the house which I am about to build will be great and wonderful.
> — *2 Chronicles 2:7,9*

The biggest problem here is that this replica was built within 30 years of landing in the New World. At most the Jewish population would have been about 2-3 dozen, which is a fraction of the manpower that was needed to build the original temple in Jerusalem.

Two battles, One hill

The Book of Mormon narrative repeats itself in a fantastical way. It tells of two races 800 years apart who go to war and are exterminated, save one person, who lives to tell about it.

	Jaredites	**Nephites and Lamanites**
Timeline	Migrated to the New World about 2500 B.C.	Migrated to the New World about 610 B.C. Lamanites split from Nephites.
All inhabitants gather for war	Ether 15:12,15	Mormon 6:2,5
Battle at Hill Cumorah	Ether 15:11 Called Ramah by Jaredites	Mormon 6:2
Extinction: only one survivor	Omni 1:21 Jaredites become extinct	Mormon 8:2-3 Lamanites annihilate Nephites

Conclusion

The Book of Mormon absurdities demonstrate the carelessness of its human origins.

King James English in the Book of Mormon

An oddity in the Book of Mormon, published in 1830, is that it uses antiquated English resembling the style of the King James Version (KJV) Bible.

Joseph Smith's other writings, such as his history and diary, reflect the Modern English Era of his day. Thus the Book of Mormon was deliberately written to read like the antiquated KJV.

Overkill: the King James Versionization of the Book of Mormon

Skeptics say the author tried too hard to make the narrative read like the KJV.

> The author labored to give his words and phrases the quaint old fashioned sound and structure of our King James translation of the scriptures. The result is a mongrel, half modern glibness and half ancient simplicity and gravity. The latter is awkward and constrained, the former natural, but grotesque by the contrast. Whenever he found his speech growing too modern, which was about every sentence or two, he labeled in a few such scriptural phrases as, "exceeding sore," "and it came to pass," etc. and made things satisfactory again. "And it came to pass," was his pet. If he had left that out, his bible would have been only a pamphlet.
> — *Mark Twain, Roughing It, p.127-128*

"and it came to pass"

Readers of the KJV will recognize this phrase. The Book of Mormon uses it proportionately 882% more than the KJV. To contrast, the phrase is used about once every 100 verses in the KJV, and about 1 in 5 verses in the Book of Mormon.

"exceedingly"

Exceedingly is used in the Book of Mormon proportionately 1,963% more than in the KJV. Other words that are magnified in frequency in the Book of Mormon when compared to the KJV.

Word	Usage	Word	Usage	Word	Usage
insomuch	2,586%	notwithstanding	558%	whoso	233%
naught	1,800%	nevertheless	536%	smitten	224%
durst	1,267%	meaneth	533%	ye	208%
beholdest	1,100%	hitherto	417%	thus	199%
inasmuch	1,033%	oft	400%	doth	191%
believest	1,000%	wherefore	355%	bringeth	175%
repenteth	850%	wax	350%	hearken	167%
beheld	711%	whoredomes	300%	iniquity	152%
didst	633%	nay	259%	wroth	150%

In his zeal to make the narrative antiquated, the author went overboard in adding "-est", "-eth", "-st", etc.

advocateth	allotteth	atoneth	awaiteth	beginneth
beheldest	beholdest	cheateth	claimeth	comprehendeth
confoundeth	counseleth	covenanteth	decreeth	deniest
enacteth	exlaimeth	fulfilleth	granteth	shouldst
manifesteth	mattereth	mingleth	murdereth	sweepeth
numbereth	overpowereth	pretendeth	scorcheth	turneth
showeth	spouteth	spurneth	supposeth	
swelleth	tortureth	trampleth	transformeth	
whispereth	wondereth	wouldst	yoketh	

Wordiness

We would expect the Book of Mormon to be efficient in words for several reasons

- The size and composition of the plates
- It claims to be an abridgement of abridgements
- The difficulty of engraving characters in ancient times

> Now behold, it came to pass that I, Jacob, having ministered much unto my people in word, (and I cannot write but a little of my words, because of the difficulty of engraving our words upon plates) and we know that the things which we write upon plates must remain.
>
> — *Jacob 4:1*

However we find just the opposite. For comparison:

	Book of Mormon	**New Testament (KJV)**
Verses	6,604	7,957
Words per verse	40.6	22.7
Total word count	268,163	180,552

Examples of its long-windedness

> And now it came to pass that all this was done in Mormon, yea, by the waters of Mormon, in the forest that was near the waters of Mormon; yea, the place of Mormon, the waters of Mormon, the forest of Mormon, how beautiful are they to the eyes of them who there came to the knowledge of their Redeemer; yea, and how blessed are they, for they shall sing to his praise forever.
>
> — *Mosiah 18:30*

And thus did the thirty and eighth year pass away, and also the thirty and ninth, and forty and first, and the forty and second, yea, even until forty and nine years had passed away, and also the fifty and first, and the fifty and second; yea, and even until fifty and nine years had passed away.

— *4 Nephi 1:6*

Anachronisms

"Anachronism: an error in chronology in which a person, object, event, etc., is assigned to a date or period other that the correct one."

— Dictionary.com

Timeline

600 BC	300 BC	421 AD	1492 AD	1611 AD	1830 AD
Jews exiled to Babylon and learn Aramaic. Book of Mormon: small group of Jews flee to New World.	Hellenization: Alexander the Great's conquest results in Greek influence over Israel. Koine Greek replaces Hebrew and Aramaic as the primary language of Jews.	Book of Mormon narrative ends.	Christopher Columbus discovers the New World	King James translation of the biblical texts published.	Book of Mormon published.

Joseph Smith claimed that the Book of Mormon is his translation of a book written in reformed Egyptian engraved on gold plates, which is a historical record of the ancient inhabitants of the Americas. The narrative dates itself from the Tower of Babel to about 421 AD.

Animals

Cattle, Oxen, Ass	There is no evidence that cattle, oxen, or ass inhabited the New World prior to European contact.
Elephants	Elephants are only native to Asia and Africa. Mastodons and mammoths became extinct during the Ice Age.
Goats, Sheep	Goats were first introduced on the American continent by Europeans in the 15th century.
Horses	North American horses became extinct around the same time as wooly mammoths, and were reintroduced in the Americas in the 1500's by the Spanish.

| Swine | There is no evidence of swine in the Americas prior to European contact. |
| | Ether 9:18 says: "swine is useful for the food of man". The Book of Mormon author must have forgotten that God forbade the Jews to eat pig (Leviticus 11:7, Deuteronomy 14:8, Isaiah 66:17) |

Agriculture

Barley	Barley did not exist in the Americas before European contact.
Figs	Figs were not native to the Americas during Book of Mormon times.
Silk	Silk comes from the Asian moth Bombyx mori, unknown to the pre-Columbian Americas.
Wheat	Wheat was introduced to the Americas by the Europeans.

Industry

Chariots	There is no evidence that ancient cultures used wheeled vehicles in the Americas.
Cimeters	A 15th century word for the curved, single-edged sword of Oriental origins. It is out of place for 500 B.C. American Indians.
Coinage	No pre-Columbian coinage has ever been found.
Compass	The compass was invented in China around 1100 A.D., long after the Book of Mormon ended in 421 A.D.
Steel	There is no evidence of high-temperature smelting in ancient American cultures. The narrative also mentions dross, which is smelting waste product. It also mentions swords made out of steel and cankered with rust.
Windows	Transparent glass was invented in Germany in the 11th century, long after the Book of Mormon ends in 421 A.D.

Linguistics

Greek words.

In the Book of Mormon narrative, a small group of Jews left Jerusalem for the New World in 600 B.C. From this point forward, Greek words and concepts would be unknown to them, as the Hellenization of Israel did not take place until 300 B.C.

Alpha and Omega	The first and last letters of the Greek alphabet should not be found on an authentic ancient text from the Americas.
Apostle	The Twelve Apostles were appointed by Jesus Christ around 30 A.D. The word apostle is from the Greek *apostolos*. In the Book of Mormon narrative an angel asks Nephi if he remembers the twelve apostles 600 years before Jesus was born.
Christ	Christ is from the Greek *Khristos*, which is a translation of the Hebrew *Mashiah* (Messiah/Messias), which means "anointed one". *Christ* never appears in the Hebrew Old Testament, and we only see Messias used twice in the Greek New Testament, and only when the author explains the translation: He first findeth his own brother Simon, and saith unto him, We have found the Messias, which is, being interpreted, the Christ. — *John 1:41* The woman saith unto him, I know that Messias cometh, which is called Christ: when he is come, he will tell us all things. — *John 4:25* Messiah is only mentioned twice in the entire Old Testament: Daniel 9:25-26. Yet it is used 26 times in the Book of Mormon. Further dating itself as a modern work: - Christ is used 186 times in the Book of Mormon during the Old Testament era. - In one instance, the name Jesus Christ is used two millennium before he is ever born. - In the Bible, the word Antichrist is only used in John's epistles I & II. In the Book of Mormon *Anti-Christ* is used 76 years before the birth of Christ.
Christians	In the Book of Mormon, the Jews call believers Christians 100 years before Jesus Christ was ever born.
Isabel	Isabel is a form of Elizabeth, which origin is from the Greek *Eleisabeth*.
Timothy	Timothy is from the Greek *Timotheos*.

Latin words

A selection of Latin words used in the Book of Mormon.

Bible	The word Bible is from the Latin *Biblia*. The last book of the Bible was written as late as 90 A.D. and the canonization of all the biblical books developed over time thereafter. However the Book of Mormon speaks of the *Bible* nearly 600 years before the New Testament was ever written.
Holy Ghost	The two titles Holy Ghost/Holy Spirit are a product of the King James translation of the New Testament. The word Ghost comes from the Old English *gast*, of which the King James often, but not always renders the Greek words *hagios* (holy) *pneuma* (spirit) as Holy Ghost. The King James is not consistent in its translation though, for example in Luke 11:13 *hagios pneuma* is rendered *Holy Spirit*. We would not expect to see an 1830 translation of an ancient text produce the same two title traits unique to the King James New Testament, but alas in the Book of Mormon we do. *Holy Spirit* is used 15 times and *Holy Ghost* 84 times. The Book of Mormon even uses both titles in the same sentence! ...and deny the good word of Christ, and the power of God, and the gift of the Holy Ghost, and quench the Holy Spirit, and make a mock of the great plan of redemption... — *Jacob 6:8*
Religion	From the Latin *religio*. Not found in the Hebrew Old Testament but used 10 times in the Book of Mormon, as early as 72 B.C. 44:5 ...by our faith, by our religion, and by our rites of worship, and by our church, and by the sacred support which we owe to our wives and our children, by that liberty which binds us to our lands and our country; yea, and also by the maintenance of the sacred word of God, to which we owe all our happiness... 48:13 ...and he had sworn with an oath to defend his people, his rights, and his country, and his religion... 51:6 ...for the freemen had sworn or covenanted to maintain their rights and the privileges of their religion by a free government... — *Alma 44:5, 48:13, 51:6* In addition, are these the words of native Indians of 72 B.C. or American Founding Fathers of 1776 AD?
Revelation	From the Latin *revelatio*. Not found in the Hebrew Old Testament but 31 times in the Book of Mormon, as early as 588 B.C.

- Joseph Smith admitted that Greek and Latin were not on the gold plates.

> There was no Greek or Latin upon the plates from which I, through the grace of God, translated the Book of Mormon. Let the language of that book speak for itself.
> — Joseph Smith, Mormonism founder, *Times and Seasons, Vol. 4, No. 13, p.193*

Theology

A selection of concepts unique to New Testament Christianity (30 A.D.) that are mentioned and understood in the pre-Christian/OT era Book of Mormon.

Baptize / Baptism	From the Greek *baptizein*. First introduced in the Gospels with John the Baptist. Absent in the Jewish Canon or the LXX OT (Septuagint), but mentioned 58 times in the OT era Book of Mormon.
"God the Father"	The concept of God as Father is not emphasized in the Old Testament until the arrival of Jesus Christ, when he declared "Abba Father" (Mark 14:36, Romans 8:15, Galatians 4:6) in the Gospels. Thus the title God the Father is unique to the Greek New Testament and not found in the Hebrew Old Testament. The title is used seven times in the OT era Book of Mormon.
Gospel	From the Old English *godspel*, of which Jesus Christ first introduced the Greek *euangelion* ("good news") in the Gospels. Gospel is not found in the Old Testament but is used 15 times in the OT era Book of Mormon, where it was introduced 600 years before the birth of Jesus Christ.
"Kingdom of God"	The phrase *Kingdom of God* is unique to New Testament Christianity, and is not found in the Old Testament. However it used 31 times in the OT era Book of Mormon.
"Kingdom of Heaven"	The phrase *Kingdom of Heaven* is unique to Gospel of Matthew, and is not found in any other New or Old Testament book. However it is used 16 times throughout the Book of Mormon.
"Lamb of God"	The phrase *Lamb of God* is unique to the Gospel of John (John 1:29,36), and is not found in any other New or Old Testament book. However it is used 33 times throughout the Book of Mormon as early as 600 B.C.

"Mysteries of God"	The phrase *Mysteries of God* is used by the Apostle Paul once in 1 Corinthians 4:1. Paul also uses *Mystery of God* in Colossians 2:2 and John in Revelation 10:7. No other New or Old Testament books use this phrase. However the Book of Mormon uses this phrase 8 times through the Book of Mormon as early as 600 B.C.
"Son of God"	While *sons of god* is used to label angels in the Old Testament, the title Son of God is unique to the New Testament texts as a title for Jesus Christ. The Book of Mormon text uses the label 55 times and 600 years before Jesus Christ was born.
Resurrection	From the Latin *resurgere*. While the notion of coming back from the dead is found in the Old Testament texts (Psalm 17:15, Daniel 12:2, Isaiah 26:19), the resurrection as a technical concept and word is unique to the Greek New Testament. The Book of Mormon text uses *resurrection* 53 times and 600 years before the New Testament was ever written.
Once a week worship service	In Judaism worship services are held daily. The concept of a once a week worship service is unique to Christianity. Mosiah 18:25 reflects 19th century Christianity not 147 B.C. Judaism: And there was one day in every week that was set apart that they should gather themselves together to teach the people, and to worship the Lord their God, and also, as often as it was in their power, to assemble themselves together. — *Mosiah 18:25*

Plagiarizing the King James Bible

The Book of Mormon quotes anachronistically from the King James Bible.

- The Book of Acts records the apostle Peter paraphrasing Moses (Deut. 18:18-19) during his sermon at Pentecost. This happened around 60 A.D. In the Book of Mormon, around 580 B.C., Nephi claims to also quote from Moses, but instead he quotes Peter's paraphrasing of Moses verbatim, 640 years before Peter gave his sermon.

Apostle Peter (60 A.D.)	**Book of Mormon (580 B.C.)**
For Moses truly said unto the fathers, A prophet shall the Lord your God raise up unto you of your brethren, like unto me; him shall ye hear in all things whatsoever he shall say unto you. And it shall come to pass, that every soul, which will not hear that prophet, shall be destroyed from among the people. — *Acts 3:22-23*	the words of Moses, which he spake, saying: A prophet shall the Lord your God raise up unto you, like unto me; him shall ye hear in all things whatsoever he shall say unto you. And it shall come to pass that all those who will not hear that prophet shall be cut off from among the people. — *1 Nephi 22:20*

- Alma chapter 5 plagiarizes John the Baptist about 80 years before he was born.

John the Baptist (30 A.D.)	**Alma (83 B.C.)**
And now also the axe is laid unto the root of the trees: therefore every tree which bringeth not forth good fruit is hewn down, and cast into the fire. — *Matthew 3:10*	And again I say unto you, the Spirit saith: Behold, the ax is laid at the root of the tree; therefore every tree that bringeth not forth good fruit shall be hewn down and cast into the fire... — *Alma 5:52*

- Mosiah chapter 16 plagiarizes the apostle Paul, 200 years before he wrote his firsts epistle to the church at Corinth.

Apostle Paul (55 A.D.)	**Mosiah (148 B.C.)**
For this corruptible must put on incorruption, and this mortal must put on immortality. — *1 Corinthians 15:53*	Even this mortal shall put on immortality, and this corruption shall put on incorruption... — *Mosiah 16:10*

- 2 Nephi plagiarizes the apostle Paul, 600 years before he wrote his epistle to the church at Rome.

Apostle Paul (68 A.D.)	**2 Nephi (555 B.C.)**
For to be carnally minded is death; but to be spiritually minded is life and peace. — *Romans 8:6*	...to be carnally-minded is death, and to be spiritually-minded is life eternal. — *2 Nephi 9:39*

View of the Hebrews

Ethan Smith's *View of the Hebrews*, is thought to be source material for Joseph Smith's *Book of Mormon*.

LDS Historian and *Seventy* Brigham Henry Roberts (B. H. Roberts) conducted an exhaustive comparison and analysis of these two books and concluded there is merit to this criticism.

- Contrary to popular belief among LDS circles, the Book of Mormon was not the first to suggest that Jews are the ancestral origins of American Indians.

    > It is often represented by Mormon speakers and writers, that the Book of Mormon was first to represent the American Indians as descendants of the Hebrews: holding that the Book of Mormon is unique in this. The claim is sometimes still ignorantly made.
    > — B. H. Roberts, LDS church historian, *Studies of the Book of Mormon, p.323*

- Many of these works predated the publication of the Book of Mormon.

    > For years such materials as were then found and discussed, theories as to the origin of the American Indians, including "the ten lost tribes" theory of Hebrew infusion into the American race, together with frequent mention of cultural traits favorable to this supposed Hebrew infusion-all this was matter of common speculation in the literature of America, before the publication of either Priest's American Antiquities or the Book of Mormon.
    > — B. H. Roberts, LDS church historian, *Studies of the Book of Mormon, p.152*

- Joseph Smith had access to these early works.

> It is altogether probable that these two books—Priest's Wonders of Nature and Providence, 1824; and Ethan Smith's View of the Hebrews 1st edition 1823, and the 2nd edition 1825—were either possessed by Joseph Smith or certainly known by him, for they were surely available to him.
> — B. H. Roberts, LDS church historian, *Studies of the Book of Mormon, p.153*

- We can confirm Joseph Smith was familiar with *View of the Hebrews* as he quoted from it.

> If such may have been the fact, that a part of the Ten Tribes came over to America, in the way we have supposed, leaving the cold regions of Assareth behind them in quest of a milder climate, it would be natural to look for tokens of the presence of Jews of some sort, along countries adjacent to the Atlantic. In order to this, we shall here make an extract from an able work: written exclusively on the subject of the Ten Tribes having come from Asia by the way of Bherings Strait, by the Rev. Ethan Smith, Pultney, Vt., who relates as follows:... -Smith's view of the Hebrews. Pg. 220.
> — Joseph Smith, Mormonism founder, *Times & Seasons, 3:813-814*

The Parallels

A summary of B. H. Roberts' comparison of View of the Hebrews and the Book of Mormon

	View of the Hebrews	**Book of Mormon**
Published	1823, first edition 1825, second edition	1830, first edition
Location	Vermont Poultney, Rutland County Note: Oliver Cowdery, one of the Book of Mormon witnesses, lived in Poultney when View of the Hebrews was published.	Vermont Sharon, Windsor County Note: Windsor County is adjacent to Rutland County.

The destruction of Jerusalem	√	√
The scattering of Israel	√	√
The restoration of the Ten Tribes	√	√
Hebrews leave the Old World for the New World	√	√
Religion a motivating factor	√	√
Migrations a long journey	√	√
Encounter "seas" of "many waters"	√	√
The Americas an uninhabited land	√	√
Settlers journey northward	√	√
Encounter a valley of a great river	√	√
A unity of race (Hebrew) settle the land and are the ancestral origin of American Indians	√	√
Hebrew the origin of Indian language	√	√
Egyptian hieroglyphics	√	√
Lost Indian records	√ A set of "yellow leaves" buried in Indian hill. Roberts noted the "leaves" may be gold.	√ Joseph Smith claims the Book of Mormon is a translation of ancient Indian records from gold plates buried in a hill.
Breastplate, Urim & Thummin	√	√
Prophets, spiritually gifted men transmit generational records	√	√
The Gospel preached in the Americas	√	√
Quotes whole chapters of Isaiah	√	√

Messiah visits the Americas	√	√
Quetzalcoatl, the white bearded Mexican "Messiah"	√	√
Good and bad are a necessary opposition	√	√
Generosity encouraged and pride denounced	√	√
Polygamy denounced	√	√
Idolatry and human sacrifice	√	√
Sacred towers and high places	√	√
Hebrews divide into two classes, civilized and barbarous	√	√
Civilized thrive in art, written language, metallurgy, navigation	√	√
Government changes from monarchy to republic	√	√
Civil and ecclesiastical power is united in the same person	√	√
Long wars break out between the civilized and barbarous	√	√
Extensive military fortifications, observations, "watch towers"	√	√
The barbarous exterminate the civilized	√	√
Discusses the United States	√	√
Ethan/Ether	Roberts noted: "Ethan is prominently connected with the recording of the matter in the one case, and Ether in the other."	
Source: B.H. Roberts, Studies of the Book of Mormon, p.240-242,324-344		

- Roberts concluded that the parallels between the two books poses a serious problem for the authenticity of Joseph Smith's Book of Mormon.

> Did Ethan Smith's *View of the Hebrews* furnish structural material for Joseph Smith's *Book of Mormon*? It has been pointed out in these pages that there are many things in the former book that might well have suggested many major things in the other. Not a few things merely, one or two, or half dozen, but many; and it is this fact of many things of similarity and the cumulative force of them that makes them so serious a menace to Joseph Smith's story of the Book of Mormon's origin.
> — B. H. Roberts, LDS church historian, *Studies of the Book of Mormon, p.240*

Isaiah in the Book of Mormon

The Book of Mormon quotes extensively from the book of Isaiah, including entire chapters, and in many cases verbatim to the King James translation. In addition to this table below, at least 52 other verses from Isaiah are found throughout the Book of Mormon.

Isaiah	Book of Mormon
Isaiah 2	2 Nephi 12
Isaiah 3	2 Nephi 13
Isaiah 4	2 Nephi 14
Isaiah 5	2 Nephi 15
Isaiah 6	2 Nephi 1
Isaiah 7	2 Nephi 17
Isaiah 8	2 Nephi 18
Isaiah 9	2 Nephi 19
Isaiah 10	2 Nephi 20
Isaiah 11	2 Nephi 21
Isaiah 12	2 Nephi 22
Isaiah 13	2 Nephi 23
Isaiah 14	2 Nephi 24
Isaiah 48	1 Nephi 20
Isaiah 49	1 Nephi 21
Isaiah 50	2 Nephi 7
Isaiah 51	2 Nephi 8
Isaiah 52	3 Nephi 20
Isaiah 53	Mosiah 14
Isaiah 54	3 Nephi 22

Plagiarism

The Book of Mormon narrative says that the Jews who left Jerusalem for the New World had with them the scriptures written up until that point (600 B.C.). That the Book of Mormon quotes from Isaiah would not be a problem, except that Joseph Smith's 1830 translation reads nearly verbatim to the 1611 King James translation. This demonstrates that he did not perform a "translation" from an ancient text written before 1611, but was merely copying from the KJV.

King James translation of Isaiah (1611)	Joseph Smith's translation of Isaiah (600 BC)
In that day the Lord will take away the **bravery of their tinkling ornaments** about their feet, and their **cauls**, and their **round tires like the moon**, The **chains**, and the **bracelets**, and the **mufflers**, The **bonnets**, and the **ornaments of the legs**, and the **headbands**, and the **tablets**, and the **earrings**, The **rings**, and **nose jewels**, The **changeable suits of apparel**, and the **mantles**, and the **wimples**, and the **crisping pins**, The **glasses**, and the **fine linen**, and the **hoods**, and the **vails**. — *Isaiah 3:18-23 (KJV)*	In that day the Lord will take away the **bravery of their tinkling ornaments**, and **cauls**, and **round tires like the moon**, The **chains** and the **bracelets**, and the **mufflers**, The **bonnets**, and the **ornaments of the legs**, and the **headbands**, and the **tablets**, and the **earrings**, The **rings**, and **nose jewels**, The **changeable suits of apparel**, and the **mantles**, and the **wimples**, and the **crisping pins**, The **glasses**, and the **fine linen**, and **hoods**, and the **vails**. — *2 Nephi 13:18-23*

KJV italicized words

The King James translation inserted additional words not found in the original texts to help clarify its translation. The KJV distinguished the additional words by italicizing them. We would not expect the Book of Mormon, which was allegedly completed by 421 A.D., to include the identical words that the KJV added centuries later. Yet we see this effect throughout the Book of Mormon.

Isaiah 9:1 (KJV)	2 Nephi 19:1
Nevertheless the dimness *shall* not *be* such as *was* in her vexation, when at the first he lightly afflicted the land of Zebulun and the land of Naphtali, and afterward did more grievously afflict her *by* the way of the sea, beyond Jordan, in Galilee of the nations. — *Isaiah 9:1 KJV*	Nevertheless, the dimness **shall** not **be** such as **was** in her vexation, when at first he lightly afflicted the land of Zebulun, and the land of Naphtali, and afterwards did more grievously afflict **by** the way of the <u>Red</u> Sea beyond Jordan in Galilee of the nations. — *2 Nephi 19:1*

In this example, 2 Nephi 9:1, dated in the Book of Mormon to be around 550 B.C., quotes nearly verbatim from the 1611 A.D. translation of Isaiah 9:1 and includes the words added (italicized) by the KJV.

Furthermore, Joseph qualified the sea as the *Red Sea*. This creates another problem in that (a) Jesus Christ quoted Isaiah in Matt. 4:14-15 and did not mention the Red sea, (b) "Red" sea is not found in any source manuscripts, (c) the Red Sea is 250 miles away!

Malachi 3:10 (KJV)	3 Nephi 24:10
...and pour you out a blessing, that *there shall* not *be room* enough *to receive it*. — *Malachi 3:10 KJV*	...and pour you out a blessing that **there shall** not **be room** enough **to receive it**. — *3 Nephi 24:10*

In this example, the KJV added seven italicized words not found in the source Hebrew manuscripts. The Book of Mormon, which was allegedly completed 1,200 years prior, contains the identical seven words.

KJV translation errors

Our understanding of the Hebrew language today is much more advanced than it was in the 1600's when King James authorized an English translation of the Bible. Somehow the divine process guiding Joseph's "translation" of the Book of Mormon didn't prevent him from making identical translation errors.

Isaiah 2:16 (KJV)	2 Nephi 12:16
And upon all the ships of Tarshish, and upon all pleasant **pictures**. — *Isaiah 2:16 KJV*	...and upon all the ships of Tarshish, and upon all pleasant **pictures**. — *2 Nephi 12:16*

In this example, where the KJV uses "pictures", the correct translation should be "crafts", or "vessels", which also fits the context better. Compare Isaiah 2:16 in the NASB and NIV

If Joseph was truly translating an ancient text by "the gift and power of God", its inexplicable that he would make the identical errors of the KJV. This is evidence that Joseph was not translating at all but merely copying from a King James Bible.

Other Points

- The name "Lucifer" comes from an improper translation in the King James Version. The name only appears once in Isaiah 14:12. Modern translations correct this, as the passage does not refer to the devil, but to the king of Babylon.
- Considering the size of the gold plates, all of the abridging, and the difficulty of engraving characters on the plates—the extensive use of Isaiah must be considered filler.
- Some scholars believe that Isaiah chapters 40 through 55 were written during the Babylonian captivity, thus after when the Jews in the Book of Mormon left Jerusalem for the New World. If true, then quotations from these chapters would be anachronistic.

Should I pray about the Book of Mormon?

Mormons appeal to Moroni 10:4 for the criteria to determine if the Book of Mormon is true.

> And when ye shall receive these things, I would exhort you that ye would ask God, the Eternal Father, in the name of Christ, if these things are not true; and if ye shall ask with a sincere heart, with real intent, having faith in Christ, he will manifest the truth of it unto you, by the power of the Holy Ghost.
> — *Moroni 10:4*

Notice that this verse already presumes that the book is true. Thus if you don't receive a feeling of its truthfulness, your prayer must not have been sincere enough.

- Feelings based confirmation is the foundation of all Mormon truth.
- Mormons are discouraged from examining the origins and particulars of their religion, but have no problems scrutinizing the Bible and other Christian denominations.
- A feelings based criteria provides no way to arbitrate between different groups that claim to receive confirmative feelings about their own religion.
- Since many churches consider the Book of Mormon scripture, even if one receives a testimony of the Book of Mormon, it itself provides no direction as to which church to join.
- Since the Book of Mormon claims to be an authentic historical record—of people, places, things, dates, and events—these underlying facts can and should be examined. Spiritual experiences are subjective and cannot be relied upon exclusively to determine if the Book of Mormon is a work of fact or fiction.

The Biblical criteria: Faith + Facts

Aside from the experiential, the Bible instructs us to study, test and prove what is true.

- *Pisteuo* is the Greek word for "believe", such as used in John 3:16, which means: *"to think to be true, to be persuaded of, an acknowledgement of fact or event, intellectual faith"*.

> Prove all things; hold fast that which is good.
> — *1 Thessalonians 5:21*

> Study to shew thyself approved unto God, a workman that needeth not to be ashamed, rightly dividing the word of truth.
> — *2 Timothy 2:15*

> Beloved, do not believe every spirit, but test the spirits to see whether they are from God, because many false prophets have gone out into the world.
> — *1 John 4:1*

We must have good reason that the Book of Mormon is an authentic historical record before we pray about its alleged spiritual truthfulness.

Otherwise, is the Book of Mormon true without prayer?

Doctrine and Covenants

A collection of revelations given primarily by Joseph Smith, and a few others. Part of the *Standward Works*.

Significant changes to the Doctrine and Covenants

- **Lectures on Faith**

    For 86 years the lectures were part of the canon until they were removed in 1921. The lectures reflect Joseph's earlier monotheistic views before they evolved into polytheism.

- **Section 2**

    Section 2 is absent in the first two editions (1833, 1835), and was inserted and back dated to make it seem that the angel Moroni had promised the priesthood in 1823.

- **Section 5**

    When Joseph wanted to be the Prophet, Seer and Revelator of the church, the original revelation was later edited to remove its restriction that Joseph would only have one gift: to translate the Book of Mormon.

- **Section 13**

    This "revelation" that Joseph Smith received the Aaronic Priesthood is not in any of the earliest editions of the Doctrine and Covenants. In fact it wasn't published until 13 years after the event and back dated to May 15, 1829.

- **Section 20**

    Three verses were added to the original revelation on church organization concerning the priesthood.

- **Section 27**

    The original revelation was edited to insert language that Joseph Smith had already received the priesthood years earlier.

- **Section 48**

    The original revelation was edited to insert the word presidency, an office the Bible and Book of Mormon do not mention.

- **Section 101**

    For 41 years this revelation explicitly prohibiting polygamy was part of the canon until it was removed in 1876 to make room for Section 132 endorsing polygamy.

Lectures on Faith

For 86 years the Lectures were part of the LDS canon until they were removed without notice in 1921. Joseph approved that the lectures were to be part of the canon as he considered them doctrine.

> During the month of January, I was engaged in the school of the Elders, and in preparing the lectures on theology for publication in the book of Doctrine and Covenants, which the committee appointed last September were now compiling.
> — Joseph Smith, Mormonism founder, *History of the Church 2:180*

> A general assembly of the Church of Latter-day Saints was held at Kirtland on the 17th of August, 1835, to take into consideration the labors of a committee appointed by a general assembly of the Church on the 24th of September, 1834, for the purpose of arranging the items of the doctrine of Jesus Christ for the government of the Church. The names of the committee were: Joseph Smith, Jun., Sidney Rigdon, Oliver Cowdery and Frederick G. Williams, who, having finished said book according to the instructions given them, deem it necessary to call a general assembly of the Church to see whether the book be approved or not by the authorities of the Church... [p.243]

> Elder John Smith, taking the lead of the High Council in Kirtland, bore record that the revelations in said book were true, and that <u>the lectures were judiciously arranged and compiled, and were profitable for doctrine</u>. Whereupon, the High Council of Kirtland accepted and acknowledged them as the doctrine and covenants of their faith by a unanimous vote.
> — Joseph Smith, Mormonism founder, *History of the Church 2:243-244*

The first part of the book will be found to contain a series of Lectures as delivered before a Theological class in this place, and <u>in consequence of their embracing the important doctrine of salvation</u>, we have arranged them into the following work.
— Joseph Smith, Mormonism founder, *Doctrine and Covenants, preface, 1835*
by Joseph Smith, Oliver Cowdery, Sidney Rigdon and F. G. Williams

Now these statements that I now read were in part written by the Prophet and in whole approved by him and taught by him in the school of the prophets. They're taken from the Lectures on Faith... this in effect is a creed announcing what Deity is. And in my judgment, it is the most comprehensive, intelligent, inspired utterance that now exists in the English language—that exists in one place defining, interpreting, expounding, announcing, and testifying what kind of a being God is. It was written by the power of the Holy Ghost, by the spirit of inspiration. And <u>it is, in effect, eternal scripture</u>; it's true.
— Bruce R. McConkie, Mormon apostle, *The Lord God of Joseph Smith, discourse delivered January 4, 1972*

Lecture V

Lecture V, which teaches Joseph's pre-polytheistic doctrine, is thought to be the primary reason why the LDS church removed the lectures from the canon in 1921.

LECTURE FIFTH

Of Faith.

SECTION V

[Lec 5:1a] In our former lectures we treated of the being, character, perfections, and attributes of God.

[Lec 5:1b] What we mean by perfections is, the perfections which belong to all the attributes of his nature.

[Lec 5:1c] We shall in this lecture speak of the Godhead; we mean the Father, Son, and Holy Spirit.

[Lec 5:2a] <u>There are two personages</u> who constitute the great, matchless, governing, and supreme power over all things - by whom all things were created and made that are created and made, whether visible or invisible;

[Lec 5:2b] whether in heaven, on earth, or in the earth, under the earth, or throughout the immensity of space.

[Lec 5:2c] They are the Father and the Son: <u>The Father being a personage of spirit</u>, glory, and power, possessing all perfection and fullness.

[Lec 5:2d] The Son, who was in the bosom of the Father, a personage of tabernacle, made or fashioned like unto man, or being in the form and likeness of man - or rather, man was formed after his likeness and in his image.

[Lec 5:2e] He is also the express image and likeness of the personage of the Father, possessing all the fullness of the Father, or the same fullness with the Father, being begotten of him;

[Lec 5:2f] and was ordained from before the foundation of the world to be a propitiation for the sins of all those who should believe on his name;

[Lec 5:2g] and <u>is called the Son because of the flesh</u> - and descended in suffering below that which man can suffer, or in other words, suffered greater sufferings, and was exposed to more powerful contradictions than any man can be.

[Lec 5:2h] But notwithstanding all this, he kept the law of God and remained without sin; showing thereby that it is in the power of man to keep the law and remain also without sin.

[Lec 5:2i] And also, that by him a righteous judgment might come upon all flesh, and that all who walk not in the law of God, may justly be condemned by the law, and have no excuse for their sins.

[Lec 5:2j] And he being the Only Begotten of the Father, full of grace and truth, and having overcome, received a fullness of the glory of the Father - <u>possessing the same mind with the Father</u>;

[Lec 5:2k] <u>which Mind is the Holy Spirit</u>, that bears record of the Father and the Son;

[Lec 5:2L] and these three are one, or in other words, these three constitute the great, matchless, governing, and supreme power over all things; by whom all things were created and made, that were created and made:

[Lec 5:2m] and these three constitute the Godhead and are one: <u>the Father and the Son possessing the same mind</u>, the same wisdom, glory, power, and fullness;

[Lec 5:2n] filling all in all -<u>the Son being filled with</u> the fullness of the Mind, glory, and power; or in other words <u>the Spirit</u>, glory, and power <u>of the Father</u> - possessing all knowledge and glory, and the same kingdom;

[Lec 5:2o] sitting at the right hand of power, in the express image and likeness of the Father - a Mediator for man - <u>being filled with the fullness of the Mind of the Father, or in other words, the Spirit of the Father</u>;

[Lec 5:2p] which Spirit is shed forth upon all who believe on his name and keep his commandments;

[Lec 5:2q] and all those who keep his commandments shall grow up from grace to grace, and become heirs of the heavenly kingdom, and joint heirs with Jesus Christ;

[Lec 5:2r] possessing the same mind, being transformed into the same image or likeness, even the express image of him who fills all in all;

[Lec 5:2s] being filled with the fullness of his glory, and become one in him, even as the Father, Son, and Holy Spirit are one.

[Lec 5:3a] From the foregoing account of the Godhead, which is given in his revelations, the saints have a sure foundation laid for the exercise of faith unto life and salvation,

[Lec 5:3b] through the atonement and mediation of Jesus Christ, by whose blood they have a forgiveness of sins, and also a sure reward laid up for them in heaven -

[Lec 5:3c] even that of partaking of the fullness of the Father and the Son, through the Spirit.

[Lec 5:3d] As the Son partakes of the fullness of the Father through the Spirit, so the saints are, by the same Spirit, to be partakers of the same fullness, to enjoy the same glory;

[Lec 5:3e] for as the Father and the Son are one, so in like manner the saints are to be one in them through the love of the Father, the mediation of Jesus Christ, and the gift of the Holy Spirit;

[Lec 5:3f] they are to be heirs of God and joint heirs with Jesus Christ.

Doctrine and Covenants Section 2

This revelation was not published in the first two editions (1833 and 1835). The earliest record of Joseph Smith ever mentioning the angel Moroni dates to 1835. Modern editions contain Section 2, which is back dated making it appear that the angel Moroni had promised the priesthood in 1823.

1 Behold, <u>I will reveal unto you the Priesthood</u>, by the hand of Elijah the prophet, before the coming of the great and dreadful day of the Lord.

2 And he shall plant in the hearts of the children the promises made to the fathers, and the hearts of the children shall turn to their fathers.

3 If it were not so, the whole earth would be utterly wasted at his coming.

Doctrine and Covenants Section 5

When Joseph Smith claimed to have received a revelation to be *Prophet, Seer and Revelator* of the church, the original revelation of Section 5 was edited to remove the restriction that Joseph's only gift would be to translate the Book of Mormon. Apparently God changed his mind.

Book of Commandments 4:2	**Doctrine and Covenants 5:4**
And he has a gift to translate the book, and I have commanded him that he shall pretend to no other gift, for I will grant him no other gift.	And you have a gift to translate the plates; <u>and this is the first gift that I bestowed upon you</u>; and I have commanded that you should pretend to no other gift <u>until my purpose is fulfilled in this</u>; for I will grant unto you no other gift <u>until it is finished</u>.

Doctrine and Covenants Section 13

This "revelation" was first published in Times & Seasons in 1842, 13 years after the event allegedly occurred, and back dated to May 15, 1829. It was canonized in the Doctrine & Covenants in 1876.

> *Ordination of Joseph Smith and Oliver Cowdery to the Aaronic Priesthood along the bank of the Susquehanna River, near Harmony, Pennsylvania, May 15, 1829. HC 1: 39–42. The ordination was done by the hands of an angel, who announced himself as John, the same that is called John the Baptist in the New Testament. The angel explained that he was acting under the direction of Peter, James, and John, the ancient apostles, who held the keys of the higher priesthood, which was called the Priesthood of Melchizedek. The promise was given to Joseph and Oliver that in due time the Priesthood of Melchizedek would be conferred upon them.*
>
> 1 Upon you my fellow servants, in the name of Messiah I confer the Priesthood of Aaron, which holds the keys of the ministering of angels, and of the gospel of repentance, and of baptism by immersion for the remission of sins; and this shall never be taken again from the earth, until the sons of Levi do offer again an offering unto the Lord in righteousness.

There is no record that Joseph Smith or Oliver Cowdery ever received the Melchizedek priesthood.

> The promise to confer upon Joseph and Oliver the Melchisedek Priesthood was fulfilled; but as there is no definite account of the event in the history of the Prophet Joseph, or, for matter of that, in any of our annals.
>
> — B. H. Robert, LDS church historian, *History of the Church 1:40*

Doctrine and Covenants Section 20

The original revelation, dated June, 1830, was later edited to insert (vv. 65 to 67) language about the priesthood. The current section heading now dates this revelation to April, 1830, in conformity with the organization of the church.

Book of Commandments Chapter XXIV (1833)	Doctrine and Covenants Section 20
The Articles and Covenants of the church of Christ, given in Fayette, New-York, June, 1830.	Revelation on Church organization and government, given through Joseph Smith the Prophet, April 1830.
	65 No person is to be ordained to any office in this church, where there is a regularly organized branch of the same, without the vote of that church; 66 But the presiding elders, traveling bishops, high councilors, high priests, and elders, may have the privilege of ordaining, where there is no branch of the church that a vote may be called. 67 Every president of the high priesthood (or presiding elder), bishop, high councilor, and high priest, is to be ordained by the direction of a high council or general conference.

Doctrine and Covenants Section 27

The original revelation was edited later to insert language that Joseph Smith had already received the priesthood years earlier.

Book of Commandments, Chapter XXVIII	Doctrine & Covenants, Section 27
A Commandment to the church of Christ, given in Harmony, Pennsylvania, September 4, 1830.	Revelation given to Joseph Smith the Prophet, at Harmony, Pennsylvania, August 1830.
6 Behold this is wisdom in me, wherefore marvel not, for the hour cometh that I will drink of the fruit of the vine with you, on the earth, and with all those whom my Father hath given me out of the world:	5 Behold, this is wisdom in me; wherefore, marvel not, for the hour cometh that I will drink of the fruit of the vine with you on the earth, and with Moroni, whom I have sent unto you to reveal the Book of Mormon, containing the fulness of my everlasting gospel, to whom I have committed the keys of the record of the stick of Ephraim; 6 And also with Elias, to whom I have committed the keys of bringing to pass the restoration of all things spoken by the mouth of all the holy prophets since the world began, concerning the last days; 7 And also John the son of Zacharias, which Zacharias he (Elias) visited and gave promise that he should have a son, and his name should be John, and he should be filled with the spirit of Elias; 8 Which John I have sent unto you, my servants, Joseph Smith, Jun., and Oliver Cowdery, to ordain you unto the first priesthood which you have received, that you might be called and ordained even as Aaron; 9 And also Elijah, unto whom I have committed the keys of the power of turning the hearts of the fathers to the children, and the hearts of the children to the fathers, that the whole earth may not be smitten with a curse; 10 And also with Joseph and Jacob, and Isaac, and Abraham, your fathers, by whom the promises remain; 11 And also with Michael, or Adam, the father of all, the prince of all, the ancient of days; 12 And also with Peter, and James, and John, whom I have sent unto you, by whom I have ordained you and confirmed you to be apostles, and especial witnesses of my name, and bear the keys of your ministry and of the same things which I revealed unto them; 13 Unto whom I

	have committed the keys of my kingdom, and a dispensation of the gospel for the last times; and for the fulness of times, in the which I will gather together in one all things, both which are in heaven, and which are on earth; 14 And also with all those whom my Father hath given me out of the world.
7 Wherefore lift up your hearts and rejoice, and gird up your loins and be faithful until I come:—even so. Amen.	15 Wherefore, lift up your hearts and rejoice, and gird up your loins, and take upon you my whole armor, that ye may be able to withstand the evil day, having done all, that ye may be able to stand. 16 Stand, therefore, having your loins girt about with truth, having on the breastplate of righteousness, and your feet shod with the preparation of the gospel of peace, which I have sent mine angels to commit unto you; 17 Taking the shield of faith wherewith ye shall be able to quench all the fiery darts of the wicked; 18 And take the helmet of salvation, and the sword of my Spirit, which I will pour out upon you, and my word which I reveal unto you, and be agreed as touching all things whatsoever ye ask of me, and be faithful until I come, and ye shall be caught up, that where I am ye shall be also. Amen.

Doctrine and Covenants Section 48

The original revelation was edited later to insert the word *presidency*. The Bible and Book of Mormon are silent on such a church office.

Book of Commandments, Chapter LI (1833)	Doctrine & Covenants, Section 48
A Revelation to the bishop, and the church in Kirtland, given in Kirtland, Ohio, March, 1831.	Revelation given through Joseph Smith the Prophet, at Kirtland, Ohio, March 1831.
6 And then ye shall begin to be gathered with your families, every man according to his family, according to his circumstances, and as is appointed to him by the bishop and elders of the church, according to the laws and commandments, which ye have received, and which ye shall hereafter receive; even so: Amen.	6 ...and then ye shall begin to be gathered with your families, every man according to his family, according to his circumstances, and as is appointed to him by <u>the presidency and</u> the bishop ~~and elders~~ of the church, according to the laws and commandments, which ye have received, and which ye shall hereafter receive; even so. Amen

Doctrine and Covenants Section 101

The modern Mormon doctrine that temple weddings are essential was not taught in the Mormon church for at least its first 40 years. Furthermore, for 41 years this revelation prohibiting polygamy was part of the LDS canon. In 1876 it was removed and Section 132 was inserted endorsing polygamy.

ON MARRIAGE.

According to the custom of all civilized nations, marriage is regulated by laws and ceremonies: therefore we believe, that all marriages in this church of Christ of Latter Day Saints, should be solemnized in a public meeting, or feast, prepared for that purpose: and that the solemnization should be performed by a presiding high priest, high priest, bishop, elder, or priest, not even prohibiting those persons who are desirous to get married, of being married by other authority.-We believe that it is not right to prohibit members of this church from marrying out of the church, if it be their determination so to do, but such persons will be considered weak in the faith of our Lord and Savior Jesus Christ.

Marriage should be celebrated with prayer and thanksgiving; and at the solemnization, the persons to be married, standing together, the man on the right, and the woman on the left, shall be addressed, by the person officiating, as he shall be directed by the holy Spirit; and if there be no legal objections, he shall say, calling each by their names: "You both mutually agree to be each other's companion, husband and wife, observing the legal rights belonging to this condition; that is, keeping yourselves wholly for each other, and from all others, during your lives." And when they have answered "Yes," he shall pronounce them "husband and wife" in the name of the Lord Jesus Christ, and by virtue of the laws of the country and authority vested in him: "may God add his blessings and keep you to fulfill your covenants from henceforth and forever. Amen."

The clerk of every church should keep a record of all marriages, solemnized in his branch.

All legal contracts of marriage made before a person is baptized into this church, should be held sacred and fulfilled. Inasmuch as this church of Christ has been reproached with the crime of fornication, and polygamy: we declare that we believe, that one man should have one wife; and one woman, but one husband, except in case of death, when either is at liberty to marry again. It is not right to persuade a woman to be baptized contrary to the will of her husband, neither is it lawful to influence her to leave her husband. All children are bound by law to obey their parents; and to influence them to embrace any religious faith, or be baptized, or leave their parents without their consent, is unlawful and unjust. We believe that husbands, parents and masters who exercise control over their wives, children, and servants and prevent them from embracing the truth, will have to answer for that sin.

Note: when D&C 101 was reprinted in the Times and Seasons, Vol. III, No. 23, October 1, 1842, p.939, the following was added:

We have given the above rule of marriage as the only one practiced in this church, to show that Dr. J. C. Bennett's "secret wife system" is a matter of his own manufacture; and further to disabuse the public ear, and shew [show] that the said Bennett and his misanthropic friend Origen Bachelor, are perpetrating a foul and infamous slander upon an innocent people, and need but be known to be hated and despise. In support of this position, we present the following certificates:-

We the undersigned members of the church of Jesus Christ of Latter-Day Saints and residents of the city of Nauvoo, persons of families do hereby certify and declare that we know of no other rule or system of marriage than the one published from the Book of Doctrine and Covenants, and we give this certificate to show that Dr. J. C. Bennett's "secret wife system" is a creature of his own make as we know of no such society in this place nor never did.

S. Bennett, N. K. Whitney,

George Miller, Albert Pettey,

Alpheus Cutler, Elias Higbee,

Reynolds Cahoon, John Taylor,

Wilson Law, E. Robinson,

W. Woodruff, Aaron Johnson.

We the undersigned members of the ladies' relief society, and married females do certify and declare that we know of no system of marriage being practised [practiced] in the church of Jesus Christ of Latter Day Saints save the one contained in the Book of Doctrine and Covenants, and we give this certificate to the public to show that J. C. Bennett's "secret wife system" is a disclosure of his own make.

Emma Smith, President,

Elizabeth Ann Whitney, Counsellor,

Sarah M. Cleveland, Counsellor,

Eliza R. Snow, Secretary,

Mary C. Miller, Catharine Pettey,

Lois Cutler, Sarah Higbee,

Thirza Cahoon, Phebe Woodruff

Ann Hunter, Leonora Taylor,

Jane Law, Sarah Hillman,

Sophia R. Marks, Rosannah Marks

Pearl of Great Price

The Pearl of Great Price is a collection of various works canonized in 1880. It is considered official canon, part of the *Standard Works*.

Book of Moses

An excerpt from the *Inspired Version*—Joseph Smith's translation of the Bible, in particular the book of Genesis.

Book of Abraham

Joseph's alleged translation of Egyptian papyri he said was written by the patriarch Abraham.

Joseph Smith—Matthew

An excerpt from the *Inspired Version*—Joseph Smith's translation of the Bible, in particular the book of Matthew.

Joseph Smith—History

An extract from the *History of the Church*

Articles of Faith

The Mormon Creed

Book of Abraham

Timeline

1799	1835	1842	1844	1858	1860	1966	1967
Rosetta Stone discovered	Joseph Smith begins translating Egyptian papyri	Translation published as Book of Abraham	Papyri sold after Joseph's death	English translation of Rosetta Stone complete	Egyptologists identify Book of Abraham facsimiles as common funerary documents	Original translation papers leaked from LDS church vault and published	LDS church reacquire papyri from the Met, NY

Introduction

In the summer of 1835, a traveling exhibit of Egyptian mummies came to Joseph Smith's town. Inside the coffins in connection with two mummies were two rolls and fragments of papyri.

> On opening the coffins, he [Michael H. Chandler] discovered that in connection with two of the bodies, was something rolled up with the same kind of linen, saturated with the same bitumen, which, when examined, proved to be two rolls of papyrus, previously mentioned. Two or three other small pieces of papyrus, with astronomical calculations, epitaphs, &c., were found with others of the mummies.
> — Joseph Smith, Mormonism founder, *History of the Church 2:349*

Since Joseph claimed to have translated reformed Egyptian to produce the Book of Mormon (Mormon 9:32), and claimed to be a seer (D&C 124:125): one who can translate all records that are of ancient date (Mosiah 8:13), he was approached to translate a few characters from the papyri.

> On the 3rd of July, Michael H. Chandler came to Kirtland to exhibit some Egyptian mummies. There were four human figures, together with some two or more rolls of papyrus covered with hieroglyphic figures and devices. As Mr. Chandler had been told I could translate them, he brought me some of the characters, and I gave him the interpretation.
> — Joseph Smith, Mormonism founder, *History of the Church 2:235*

The church purchased the papyri and Joseph identified the origins of it.

> Soon after this, some of the Saints at Kirtland purchased the mummies and papyrus, a description of which will appear hereafter, and with W.W. Phelps and Oliver Cowdery as scribes, I commenced the translation of some of the characters or hieroglyphics, and much to our joy found that one of the rolls contained the writings of Abraham, another writings of Joseph of Egypt, etc.—a more full account of which will appear in its place, as I proceed to examine or unfold them. Truly we can say, the Lord is beginning to reveal the abundance of peace and truth.
> — Joseph Smith, Mormonism founder, *History of the Church 2:236*

Joseph's translation of the "Abraham roll" is published as the Book of Abraham, part of the LDS canon *Pearl of Great Price*.

Mormons believe that the characters of the papyri are written by Abraham's own hand.

> Joseph the Seer has presented us some of the Book of Abraham which was written by his own hand but hid from the knowledge of man for the last four thousand years but has now come to light through the mercy of God.
> — Wilford Woodruff, Mormon prophet, *Diary, February 19, 1842*

Joseph also told visitors.

> These receptacles Smith opened, and disclosed four human bodies, shrunken and black with age. "These are mummies," said the exhibitor. "I want you to look at that little runt of a fellow over there. He was a great man in his day. Why, that was Pharaoh Necho, King of Egypt!" Some parchments inscribed with hieroglyphics were then offered us. They were preserved under glass and handled with great respect. "That is the handwriting of Abraham, the Father of the Faithful," said the prophet. "This is the autograph of Moses, and these lines were written by his brother Aaron. Here we have the earliest account of the creation, from which Moses composed the first book of Genesis.
> — Josiah Quincy, *Figures of the Past, p.386*

Also evidenced in the introduction to the Book of Abraham.

> THE BOOK OF ABRAHAM
> TRANSLATED FROM THE PAPYRUS, BY JOSEPH SMITH
> A Translation of some ancient Records, that have fallen into our hands from the catacombs of Egypt.—The writings of Abraham while he was in Egypt, called the Book of Abraham, written by his own hand, upon papyrus.

Since Abraham lived before Moses, who wrote the Torah (the first five books of the Old Testament), it would make the Abraham papyrus older than the book of Genesis! A view endorsed by noted Mormon scholar Sidney B. Sperry.

> It is evident that the writings of Abraham while he was in Egypt, of which our printed Book of Abraham is a copy, must of necessity be older than the original text of Genesis.
> — Sidney B. Sperry, Mormon scholar, *Ancient Records Testify in Papyrus and Stone, p.83*

Verifying Joseph's Translation

The consequences are eternal: if Joseph Smith's translation of the papyri is accurate, it would confirm his claim that he possessed a supernatural gift. However, if his translation is inaccurate, then he is exposed as a false prophet who perpetuated a fraud. In that event it would cast doubt on his other "translation": the Book of Mormon.

When Joseph began translating the papyrus in 1835, no one at that time in America could verify the accuracy of it.

The Rosetta Stone was the key to deciphering Egyptian hieroglyphics. The first English translation of the stone was completed in 1858 by the Philomathean Society of Pennsylvania. Published in the Book of Abraham are three facsimiles copied from the papyrus along with Joseph's interpretations of them.

Facsimile 1   Facsimile 2   Facsimile 3

Independent Examinations

Over a dozen Egyptologists have examined the facsimiles and/or the original papyri. Their conclusions all lead to one answer: Joseph Smith was ignorant of the Egyptian script. Both LDS and non-LDS Egyptologists have identified the papyri as common Egyptian funerary documents belonging to the *Book of the Dead*, hence why the papyri were found in coffins. The papyri are dated about 1,500 years after Abraham lived.

Excerpts from Egyptologists

"... I have examined the illustrations given in the 'Pearl of Great Price.' In the first place, they are copies (very badly done) of well known Egyptian subjects of which I have dozens of examples. Secondly, they are all many centuries later than Abraham... the attempts to guess a meaning for them, in the professed explanations, are too absurd to be noticed. It may be safely said that there is not one single word that is true in these explanations... None but the ignorant could possibly be imposed on by such ludicrous blunders ..."
— Dr. W. M. Flinders Petrie, London University

"... these three fac-similes of Egyptian documents in the 'Pearl of Great Price' depict the most common objects in the mortuary religion of Egypt. Joseph Smiths' interpretation of them as part of a unique revelation through Abraham, therefore, very clearly demonstrates that he was totally unacquainted with the significance of these documents and absolutely ignorant of the simplest facts of Egyptian writing and civilization... We orientalists could publish scores of these 'fac-similes from the Book of Abraham' taken from other sources ..."
— James H. Breasted, Ph.D., Haskell Oriental Museum, Univ. of Chicago

"... the author knew neither the Egyptian language nor the meaning of the most commonplace Egyptian figures... it may be remarked that his explanations from a scientific and scholarly standpoint are absurd... the explanatory notes to his fac-similes cannot be taken seriously by any scholar, as they seem to be undoubtedly the work of pure imagination ..."
— Rev. Prof. C. A. B. Mercer, Ph. D., Western Theological Seminary, Custodian Hibbard Collection, Egyptian Reproductions

"... What he calls the 'Book of Abraham' is a funeral Egyptian text, probably not older than the Greek ages... Jos. Smith certainly never got a Divine revelation in the meaning of the ancient Egyptian Script, and that he never deciphered hieroglyphic texts at all ..."
— Dr. Friedrich von Bissing, Prof. of Egyptology, Univ. of Munich

"... The plates contained in the 'Pearl of Great Price' are rather comical and a very poor imitation of Egyptian originals... The text of this chapter, as also the interpretation of the plates, displays an amusing ignorance. Chaldeans and Egyptians are hopelessly mixed together, although as dissimilar and remote in language, religion and locality as are today American and Chinese. In addition to which the writer knows nothing of either of them ..."
— Dr. John Peters, Univ. of Pennsylvania

"... It is difficult to deal seriously with Joseph Smith's impudent fraud... I need scarce say that Kolob, etc., are unknown to the Egyptian language... Smith has turned the Goddess into a king and Osiris into Abraham ..."
— Dr. A. H. Sayce, Oxford, England

"... The 'Book of Abraham,' it is hardly necessary to say, is a pure fabrication. Cuts 1 and 3 are inaccurate copies of well known scenes on funeral papyri, and cut 2 is a copy of one of the magical discs... Joseph Smith's interpretation of these cuts is a farrago of nonsense from beginning to end. Egyptian characters can now be read almost as easily as Greek, and five minutes' study in an Egyptian gallery of any museum should be enough to convince any educated man of the clumsiness of the imposture ..."
— Dr. Arthur C. Mace, Asst. Curator, Metropolitan Museum of Art, New York, Dept. of Egyptian Art

"... The Egyptian papyrus which Smith declared to be the 'Book of Abraham,' and 'translated' or explained in his fantastical way, and of which three specimens are published in the 'Pearl of Great Price,' are parts of the well known 'Book of the Dead' ..."
— Dr. Edward Meyer, University of Berlin

"... From the standpoint of the Egyptologist the explanations given with these illustrations are incorrect. The Egyptian language on such documents is decipherable and has appeared in translation in various books ..."
— John A. Wilson, Prof. of Egyptology, University of Chicago

"... The explanations are completely wrong insofar as any interpretation of the Egyptian original is concerned ..."
— Richard Parker, Dept. of Egyptology, Brown University

Full quotes and additional examinations can be obtained online at http://www.MormonHandbook.com

Book of Abraham Facsimile 1

Common Egyptian funerary scenes. Note: the top left image is an artist's depiction of Facsimile 1 restored properly.

Joseph Smith filled in the areas where the papyrus was damaged (sketchings are seen on the source papyrus at left). Egyptologists agree these restorations are inaccurate (noted below).

Source Papyrus	As published in the Book of Abraham

Verifying Joseph's Interpretation

Figure	Joseph Smith	Egyptology
1	The Angel of the Lord. Note: this should have a human head, however the papyrus was torn off here, so Joseph penciled in a bird's head.	Isis: the sister-wife of Osiris
2	Abraham fastened on an altar.	Osiris on an embalming table wrapped in clothes for mummification
3	The idolatrous priest of Elkenah attempting to offer up Abraham as a sacrifice. Note: the head of Anibus is a jackal, however the papyrus was torn off here, so Joseph penciled in a human head.	Anubis, the Egyptian funeral god
4	The altar for sacrifice by the idolatrous priests, standing before the gods of Elkenah, Libnah, Mahmackrah, Korash, and Pharaoh.	An embalming table (aka lion's couch)
5	The idolatrous god of Elkenah. Note: there is no Egyptian god Elkenah.	These are canopic jars that contain the deceased organs, and are representative of the sons of the god Hor. This one is of Qebehseneuf, who receives the intestines.
6	The idolatrous god of Libnah. Note: there is no Egyptian god Libnah.	These are canopic jars that contain the deceased organs, and are representative of the sons of the god Hor. This one is of Duamutef, who receives the stomach.
7	The idolatrous god of Mahmackrah. Note: there is no Egyptian god Mahmackrah.	These are canopic jars that contain the deceased organs, and are representative of the sons of the god Hor. This one is of Hapy, who receives the lungs.
8	The idolatrous god of Korash. Note: there is no Egyptian god Korash.	These are canopic jars that contain the deceased organs, and are representative of the sons of the god Hor. This one is of Imsety, who receives the liver.
9	The idolatrous god of Pharaoh. Note: the word pharaoh is an anachronism, as it was not used as a title until Thutmose III (ca. 1479-1425 BC) long after Abraham's death in (1637 BC or 1801 BC).	The Egyptian god Horus or Sobek, who's head is a crocodile.

10	Abraham in Egypt.	Funeral offerings covered with lotus flowers.
11	Designed to represent the pillars of heaven, as understood by the Egyptians.	Serekh representing a gated facade of a palace, thus signifying that the ceremony took place behind the wall inside the palace.
12	Raukeeyang, signifying expanse, or the firmament over our heads; but in this case, in relation to this subject, the Egyptians meant it to signify Shaumau, to be high, or the heavens, answering to the Hebrew word, Shaumahyeem. Note: Raukeeyang and Shaumau are not Egyptian words.	Water the crocodile swims in.

Book of Abraham Facsimile 2

Facsimile 2 in the Book of Abraham is a common Egyptian hypocephalus

While we don't have the original hypocephalus, an early rendering of it reveals damage, and Egyptologists agree that Facsimile 2 is a poor and inaccurate restoration.

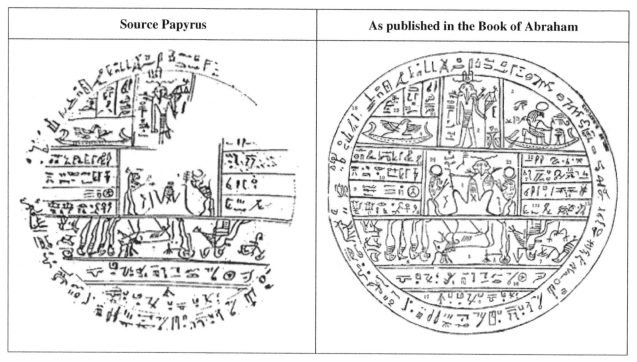

Verifying Joseph's Interpretation

Figure	Joseph Smith	Egyptology
1	Kolob, signifying the first creation, nearest to the celestial, or the residence of God. First in government, the last pertaining to the measurement of time. The measurement according to celestial time, which celestial time signifies one day to a cubit. One day in Kolob is equal to a thousand years according to the measurement of this earth, which is called by the Egyptians Jah-oh-eh. Note: Kolob and Jah-oh-eh are not Egyptian words.	The Egyptian god Khnumu.
2	Stands next to Kolob, called by the Egyptians Oliblish, which is the next grand governing creation near to the celestial or the place where God resides; holding the key of power also, pertaining to other planets; as revealed from God to Abraham, as he offered sacrifice upon an altar, which he had built unto the Lord. Note: Oliblish is not an Egyptian word.	The Egyptian god Amen-Re.
3	Is made to represent God, sitting upon his throne, clothed with power and authority; with a crown of eternal light upon his head; representing also the grand Key-words of the Holy Priesthood, as revealed to Adam in the Garden of Eden, as also to Seth, Noah, Melchizedek, Abraham, and all to whom the Priesthood was revealed.	The Egyptian god Horus-Re in a boat.
4	Answers to the Hebrew word Raukeeyang, signifying expanse, or the firmament of the heavens; also a numerical figure, in Egyptian signifying one thousand; answering to the measuring of the time of Oliblish, which is equal with Kolob in its revolution and in its measuring of time. Note: Raukeeyang and Oliblish are not Egyptian words.	The Egyptian god Sokar.
5	Is called in Egyptian Enish-go-on-dosh; this is one of the governing planets also, and is said by the Egyptians to be the Sun, and to borrow its light from Kolob through the medium of Kae-e-vanrash, which is the grand Key, or, in other words, the governing power, which governs fifteen other fixed planets or stars, as also Floeese or the Moon, the Earth and the Sun in their annual revolutions. This planet receives its power through the medium of Kli-flos-is-es, or Hah-ko-kau-beam, the stars represented by numbers 22 and 23, receiving light from the revolutions of Kolob. Note: Enish-go-on-dosh, Floeese, Kli-flos-is-es, Hah-ko-kau-beam, Kae-e-vanrash are not Egyptian words.	The cow of Hathor and behind it a goddess holding a tree.
6	Represents this earth in its four quarters.	The four sons of Horus: Imsety, Hapy, Duamutef, and Qebehsenuef.

7	Represents God sitting upon his throne, revealing through the heavens the grand Key-words of the Priesthood; as, also, the sign of the Holy Ghost unto Abraham, in the form of a dove. Note: the original phallus (erect penis) was removed in past editions of the Pearl of Great Price, and restored in the 1981 Triple Combo (KJV, D&C, PGP).	The Egyptian god Min (sitting) and Atum (a snake).
8-22	No interpretations provided.	

Book of Abraham Facsimile 3

Facsimile 3 in the Book of Abraham is a scene from the ancient Egyptian *Book of the Dead*

The source papyrus is missing or vaulted in LDS church archives.

Verifying Joseph's Interpretation

Figure	Joseph Smith	Egyptology
Above scene		Stars represent the souls of the dead.
1	Abraham sitting upon Pharaoh's throne, by the politeness of the king, with a crown upon his head, representing the Priesthood, as emblematical of the grand Presidency in Heaven; with the scepter of justice and judgment in his hand. Note: the word pharaoh is an anachronism, as it was not used as a title until Thutmose III (ca. 1479-1425 BC) long after Abraham's death in (1637 BC or 1801 BC).	The Egyptian god Osiris. The writing above Osiris: "Recitation by Osiris foremost of the westerners lord of Abydos(?) the great god forever and ever(?)".
2	King Pharaoh, whose name is given in the characters above his head.	The Egyptian goddess Isis, the wife of Osiris. The writing above Isis: "Isis the great the gods mother".
3	Signifies Abraham in Egypt as given also in Figure 10 of Facsimile No. 1.	A libation stand.
4	Prince of Pharaoh, King of Egypt, as written above the hand.	The Egyptian goddess Maat. The writing above Maat: "Maat mistress of the gods".
5	Shulem, one of the king's principal waiters, as represented by the characters above his hand.	The deceased, Osiris Hor. The writing above Osiris Hor: "The Osiris Hor justified forever".
6	Olimlah, a slave belonging to the prince. Note: Olimlah is an unknown Egyptian word.	The Egyptian God Anubis Note: The rendering is poor as the head should be that of a jackal—notice the pointed ear on top of the head. The writing above Anubis: "Recitation by Anubis who makes protection(?) foremost of the embalming booth".
Bottom scene		The writing at the bottom: "O gods of the necropolis gods of

		the caverns gods of the south north west and east grant salvation to the Osiris Hor the justified born by Taikhibit".
Comment	Additional comment on scene: Abraham is reasoning upon the principles of Astronomy, in the king's court.	

Book of Abraham - Kirtland Egyptian Papers

The Kirtland Egyptian Papers (KEP) are working documents of Joseph Smith's translation of Egyptian papyri, of which is a source for his Book of Abraham.

The manuscripts are written by Joseph Smith and his scribes.
- William W. Phelps
- Warren Parrish
- Oliver Cowdery
- Frederick G. Williams
- Willard Richards

The LDS church has never published the KEP and they remain vaulted in its archives. A microfilm copy was leaked to the Tanners of Utah Lighthouse Ministry, which is the only source of these papers today.

An overview of the papers

- **Grammar & Alphabet of Egyptian Language**

  Four manuscripts that contain Egyptian and invented characters with Joseph's English names and definitions of them. Many of the words and definitions from these documents are found in the Book of Abraham and the facsimile definitions.

  > The remainder of the month, I was continually engaged in translating an alphabet to the Book of Abraham, and arranging a grammar of the Egyptian language as practiced by the ancients.
  >
  > — Joseph Smith, Mormonism founder, *History of the Church 2:238*

- **Egyptian Counting**

    A manuscript with invented numbers, their names, and Joseph's English counterparts.

- **Translation Manuscripts**

    Three manuscripts that contain characters copied from the source papyri (Abraham roll) along with Joseph's translations of them, which comprise the text of Abraham 1:1-2:18.

Examining the Translation Manuscripts

These manuscripts copy characters from the papyrus section highlighted below (and invent characters where the papyrus is damaged or missing) along with Joseph's translation of them, which comprise the text of Abraham 1:1-2:18.

The "Abraham roll"

From the Abraham roll—to the translation manuscript—to the Book of Abraham

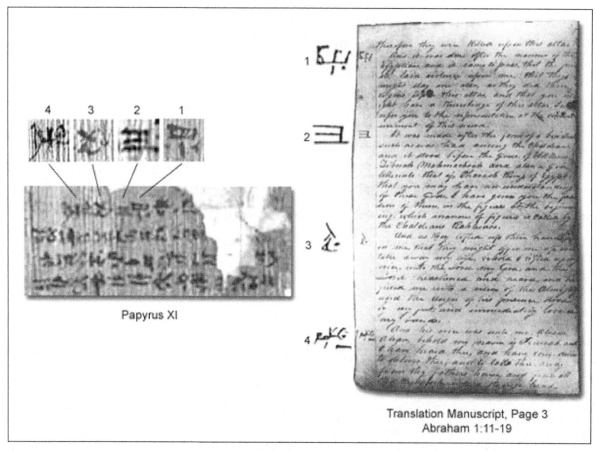

Egyptian characters are read from right to left. In this example, from page 3 of the translation manuscript, the characters from the papyrus Joseph named the Abraham roll are copied to the left margin and Joseph's interpretation of each character is written to its right. Page 3 of the manuscript comprises the Book of Abraham, chapter 1, verses 11 to 19.

Comparing Translations

This example compares Joseph's translation from page 3 of the translation manuscript.

Symbol	Papyrus	Manuscript	Joseph Smith	Egyptology
1			(1:11) manner of the Egyptians. (1:12) And it came to pass that the priests laid violence upon me, that they might slay me also, as they did those virgins upon this altar; and that you may have a knowledge of this altar, I will refer you to the representation at the commencement of this record.	"pool"
2			(1:13) It was made after the form of a bedstead, such as was had among the Chaldeans, and it stood before the gods of Elkenah, Libnah, Mahmackrah, Korash, and also a god like unto that of Pharaoh, king of Egypt. (1:14) That you may have an understanding of these gods, I have given you the fashion of them in the figures at the beginning, which manner of the figures is called by the Chaldeans Rahleenos, which signifies hieroglyphics.	"water"
3			(1:15) And as they lifted up their hands upon me, that they might offer me up and take away my life, behold, I lifted up my voice unto my God, and the Lord hearkened and heard, and he filled me with the vision of the Almighty, and the angel of his presence stood by me, and immediately unloosed my bands;	"great"
4			(1:16) And his voice was unto me: Abraham, Abraham behold, my name is Jehovah, and I have heard thee, and have come down to deliver thee, and to take thee away from thy father's house, and from all the kinsfolk, into a strange land (page 4) which thou knowest not of; (1:17) And this because they have turned their hearts away from me, to worship the god of Elkenah, and the god of Libnah, and the god of Mahmackrah, and the god of Korash, and the god of Pharaoh, king of Egypt; therefore I have come down to destroy him who hath lifted up his hand against thee, Abraham, my son, to take away thy life. (1:18) Behold, I will lead thee by my hand, and I will take thee, to put upon thee my name, even the Priesthood of thy father, and my power shall be over thee. (1:19) And it was with Noah so shall it be with thee; but through thy ministry my name shall be known in the earth forever, for I am thy God.	"Khonsu" (Egyptian moon god)

Conclusion

The Kirtland Egyptian Papers allow us to examine Joseph's accuracy in translating Egyptian characters.

Egyptoligist I.E. Stephen Edwards sums up an analysis of the KEP best:

> The whole work was, "largely a piece of imagination and lacking in any kind of scientific a value."
> — I.E.S. Edwards, Keeper of the Department of Egyptian Antiquities, British Museum, *Letter dated June 9, 1966* (as quoted in Charles M. Larson, *By His Own Hand Upon Papyrus, p. 43*)

Since the Book of Abraham is demonstrated to be a false translation, this proves Joseph Smith perpetuated a fraud and raises serious doubts about his other translation—the *Book of Mormon*.

King James Version Bible

The Holy Bible (Latin for *books*) is a collection of 66 books which contain the teachings of the prophets of the Old Covenant and the teachings of Jesus Christ and his apostles under the New Covenant. The King James Version (KJV) is a translation commissioned by King James I of England and published in 1611.

- While Mormons are permitted to read other translations, the King James is the only version canonized as part of the LDS *Standard Works*.
- Like atheists, Mormons do not consider the books of the Bible to be completely reliable. The general attitude toward the Bible is that the texts have been corrupted over the years do to an alleged apostasy.

Inspired Version

The Inspired Version, also called the Joseph Smith Translation (JST), is Joseph Smith's "translation" of the Bible, or better, his editing and rewriting of the King James Version. Joseph started the project in June, 1830 and finished July 2, 1833. He prepared a manuscript for publication but it was never published before his death. The LDS church has only canonized excerpts of it, namely Genesis (Book of Moses) and Matthew (Joseph Smith—Matthew).

Journal of Discourses

A collection of 1,438 public sermons given by 55 general authorities. While not officially canon today, General Authorities considered the journal to be part of the *Standard Works*.

> The Journal of Discourses deservedly ranks as one of the standard works of the Church, and every rightminded Saint will certainly welcome with joy every number as it comes forth.
> — George Q. Cannon, Mormon prophet, *Journal of Discourses, Volume 8, Preface*

> Each successive Volume of these Discourses is a rich mine of wealth, containing gems of great value, and the diligent seeker will find ample reward for his labor. After the fathers and mothers of this generation have made them the study of their lives their children's children will find that they are still unexhausted, and rejoice that this Record has been handed down from their fathers to also aid them in following the way of life.
> — Orson Pratt, Mormon apostle, *Journal of Discourses, Volume 3, Preface*

> It is impossible to give monetary value to the past volumes of this publication... Those who read the utterances of the servants of God, contained in this book, under the same influence by which the speakers were inspired, cannot fail to receive profit from the perusal.
> — Joseph F. Smith, Mormon prophet, *Journal of Discourses, Volume 18, Preface*

We take great pleasure in presenting to the Saints and the world... the Journal of Discourses, which they will find contains rich treasures of information concerning the glorious principles of Eternal Life, as revealed through God's anointed servants in these last days. All who read the discourses contained in this Volume are earnestly recommended to adapt them to their lives by practice, and we can confidently assure them that, in doing so, they are laying up a store of knowledge that will save and exalt them in the Celestial kingdom.
— Albert Carrington, Mormon apostle, *Journal of Discourses, Volume 15, Preface*

Other Scriptures

- LDS scripture teaches that the words of an elder when moved by the Holy Ghost are to be considered scripture.

    And whatsoever they shall speak when moved upon by the Holy Ghost shall be scripture, shall be the will of the Lord, shall be the mind of the Lord, shall be the word of the Lord, shall be the voice of the Lord, and the power of God unto salvation.
    — Doctrine and Covenants 68:4

- Brigham Young, the second and longest serving Mormon prophet, said that all of his sermons are to be considered scripture.

    I have never yet preached a sermon and sent it out to the children of men, that they may not call Scripture.
    — Brigham Young, Mormon prophet, Sermon delivered January 2, 1870 in the Salt Lake City Tabernacle, *Journal of Discourses 13:95*

Defining Mormon Doctrine

Defining what Mormons believe can be a moving target

- There is no single authoritative source as to what constitutes official LDS doctrine and official interpretation of its scripture.
- Generally the sitting Mormon prophet has the final say. This has caused doctrinal evolutions and contradictions over the years. Thus, what may be true or emphasized today may be deemed false or ignored tomorrow. Likewise, what is denied today may have been deemed true in the past. For examples see Adam/God, Polygamy, Blacks denied the priesthood, etc.
- Since Mormonism claims to be restored Christianity, the handbook only looks as those doctrines which separate Mormonism from Christianity.

The Godhead

Modern Mormonism teaches polytheism: the belief in many gods. This doctrine is aligned closer with Eastern religions than the Abrahamic faiths (Judaism, Christianity, Islam) which teach monotheism: the belief in only One God.

Monotheism - One God	Polytheism - Many gods
Judaism	Hinduism
Christianity	Buddhism
Islam	Mormonism

Since Mormonism claims to be Christian, here is a comparison of the major differences between the two:

Mormonism	Christianity
God the Father was once a mortal sinful man who ultimately obtained divinity.	God has always been Deity and created man.
God possesses a physical body of flesh and bones.	God is a spirit who transcends time, space and matter.
God is eternally progressing in knowledge and power.	God is all knowledge and power. There is no knowledge or power beyond God to acquire.
God the Father has a father, and he has a father, and so on.	God is Creator not an offspring.
God is married to Heavenly Mother(s).	God is not married.
God lives near the planet Kolob.	God is not a member within the universe but Created the universe and thus transcends it.

Jesus Christ was the first born, and Lucifer the second born son of God, thus making them brothers.	Jesus is God manifest in the flesh and the Creator of Satan.
Heavenly Father, Jesus Christ, and the Holy Ghost are three separate and distinct gods united in common purpose over this planet. This cooperation is called the Godhead.	There is only One God manifest in three persons: the Father, Son and Holy Spirit. This definition is called the Trinity. The apostles and prophets of biblical times record that God manifested as a burning bush, a pillar of fire, a cloud, an angel, a dove, as the man Jesus Christ, and even talked through a donkey. The Apostle John teaches about the *Seven Spirits* of God (Rev. 1:4, 3:1, 4:5, 5:6). Each manifestation does not require separate and distinct gods as we define it in human terms.
There are more gods beyond the Godhead.	There is only One God period.
Faithful and obedient Mormons who fulfill certain requirements may earn for themselves the ability to become their own God. This is called Exaltation.	Believers become like Jesus Christ in character (i.e. love, patient, etc.) and in some attributes (i.e. immortal, sinless, etc.) but will never become a deity or be a deity over others.
Brigham Young, the second and longest serving Mormon prophet taught that Adam is God. The LDS church denies this doctrine today.	Who God is doesn't change according on the whims of a church leader.

God Is An Exalted Man

Mormon General Authorities teach that God was not always God, but was once a mortal man.

God himself was once as we are now, and is an exalted man... I am going to tell you how God came to be God. We have imagined and supposed that God was God from all eternity. I will refute that idea... He was once a man like us; yea, that God himself, the Father of us all, dwelt on an earth.
— Joseph Smith, Mormonism founder, *Ensign, April 1971, p.13-14*

Remember that God, our heavenly Father, was perhaps once a child, and mortal like we ourselves, and rose step by step in the scale of progress, in the school of advancement; has moved forward and overcome, until He has arrived at the point where He now is.
— Orson Hyde, Mormon apostle, *Journal of Discourses 1:123*

He is our Father-the Father of our spirits, and was once a man in mortal flesh as we are, and is now an exalted Being. How many Gods there are, I do not know. But there never was a time when there were not Gods and worlds, and when men were not passing through the same ordeals that we are now passing through.
— Brigham Young, Mormon prophet, *Journal of Discourses 7:333*

God is a natural man... Where did he get his knowledge from? From his Father, just as we get knowledge from our earthly parents.
— Heber C. Kimball, First Presidency Counselor, *Journal of Discourses 8:211*

But if God the Father was not always God, but came to his present exalted position by degrees of progress as indicated in the teachings of the prophet, how has there been a God from all eternity? The answer is that there has been and there now exists an endless line of Gods, stretching back into the eternities.
— B. H. Roberts, LDS church historian, *New Witness for God 1:476*

Mormon prophets have continuously taught the sublime truth that God the Eternal Father was once a mortal man who passed through a school of earth life similar to that through which we are now passing. He became God-an exalted being. (p.104)

Yet, if we accept the great law of eternal progression, we must accept the fact that there was a time when Deity was much less powerful than He is today. (p.114)

Thus He grew in experience and continued to grow until He attained the status of Godhood. (p.115)
— Milton R. Hunter, Mormon Seventy, *The Gospel Throughout The Ages, p.104,114-15*

God is an exalted Man... The Prophet taught that our Father had a Father and so on.
— Joseph Fielding Smith, Mormon prophet, *Doctrines of Salvation 1:10,12*

God Is Eternally Progressing

Mormon prophets offer conflicting teachings if God continues to progress in knowledge and power.

God is progressing	God is not progressing
God himself is increasing and progressing in knowledge, power, and dominion, and will do so, worlds without end. — Wilford Woodruff, Mormon prophet, *Journal of Discourses 6:120* ... advancing as our Father in heaven advances, for there is progress for our father and for our Lord Jesus. There is no such thing as standing still in the eternal work of our God. It is endless progress, progressing from one degree of knowledge to another degree. — George Q. Cannon, First Presidency Counselor, *Millennial Star 61:117*	It should be realized that God is not progressing in knowledge, truth, virtue, wisdom, or any of the attributes of godliness. He has already gained these things in their fullness. — Joseph Fielding Smith, Mormon prophet cited by Bruce R. McConkie, *Mormon Doctrine, p.221 (1958)*

Christianity

The apostles and prophets of biblical times teach that God has always been God and never a man.

> You are the same and Your years will not come to an end...
> — *Psalm 102:27*

> For I, the LORD, do not change...
> — *Malachi 3:6*

> Every good thing given and every perfect gift is from above, coming down from the Father of lights, with whom there is no variation or shifting shadow.
> — *James 1:17*

> God is not a man, that He should lie...
> — *Numbers 23:19*

> The Glory of Israel will not lie or change His mind, for He is not a man that He should change His mind.
> — *1 Samuel 15:29*

> Professing to be wise, they became fools, and exchanged the glory of the incorruptible God for an image in the form of corruptible man...
> — *Romans 1:22-23*

The Book of Mormon echoes the Bible.

> For I know that God is not a partial God, neither a changeable being; but he is unchangeable from all eternity to all eternity.
> — *Moroni 8:18*

> For do we not read that God is the same yesterday, today, and forever, and in him there is no variableness neither shadow of changing?
> — *Mormon 9:9*

> For he is the same yesterday, today, and forever...
> — *1 Nephi 10:18*

God Has A Body

Both Christianity and Mormonism share the belief that Jesus Christ has a physical body, but diverge when it comes to the nature of God the Father.

Mormonism departs from the Abrahamic religions (Judaism, Christianity & Islam) that believe God is a spirit.

Jesus Christ: God is a spirit	Joseph Smith: God has a physical body
God is spirit, and those who worship Him must worship in spirit and truth. — *John 4:24* A spirit does not have flesh and bones. — *Luke 24:39*	The Father has a body of flesh and bones as tangible as man's... — Joseph Smith, Mormonism founder, *D&C 130:22*

This unique Mormon doctrine is an extension of the belief that God was formerly a mortal man.

This unique Mormon doctrine constrains God.

Christianity: God is omnipresent	Mormonism: God is not omnipresent
... the heavens and the highest heavens cannot contain Him... — *2 Chronicles 2:6* ... "Do I not fill the heavens and the earth?" declares the LORD. — *Jeremiah 23:24*	Some would have us believe that God is present everywhere. It is not so. — Brigham Young, Mormon prophet, *JoD 6:345*

Does God know everything or must rely on angels to keep him informed?

Christianity: God knows everything	Mormonism: angels keep God informed
There is no creature hidden from His sight, but all things are open and laid bare to the eyes of Him with whom we have to do. — Hebrews 4:13	He knows everything. How? When His angels and ministers tell Him of it, like any other ruler. — Orson Hyde, Mormon apostle, JoD 2:64

Does God dwell in man's heart? Note: the Book of Mormon contradicts Joseph's 1843 "revelation".

Book of Mormon (1830)	Joseph Smith, D&C 130
And this I know, because the Lord hath said he dwelleth not in unholy temples, but in the hearts of the righteous doth he dwell. — Alma 34:36	The idea that the Father and the Son dwell in a man's heart is an old sectarian notion, and is false. — Joseph Smith, Mormonism founder, D&C 130:3

Evolving doctrine

Evidence demonstrates this doctrine was introduced years later by Joseph Smith.

- Mormons cite the *First Vision*, where Joseph Smith claims to have seen God the Father appear before him in the flesh, as supportive evidence for this doctrine. But this vision wasn't published until 1842, over 20 years after the fact.
- The Book of Mormon reflects the Biblical view that God is a Spirit.

> Now this was the tradition of Lamoni, which he had received from his father, that there was a Great Spirit... and then Ammon said: Believest thou that there is a Great Spirit? And he [Lamoni] said, Yea. And Ammon said: This is God. And Ammon said unto him again: Believest thou that this Great Spirit, who is God, created all things which are in heaven and in the earth? And he [Lamoni] said: Yea...
> — Alma 18:5,26-28

> And now when Aaron heard this, his heart began to rejoice, and he said: Behold, assuredly as thou livest, O king, there is a God. And the king said: Is God that Great Spirit that brought our fathers out of the land of Jerusalem? And Aaron said unto him: Yea, he is that Great Spirit, and he created all things both in heaven and in earth. Believest thou this? And he said: Yea, I believe that the Great Spirit created all things, and I desire that ye should tell me concerning all these things, and I will believe thy words.
> — *Alma 22:8-11*

- For 86 years the Lectures on Faith were part of the LDS Canon. In 1921 the Lectures were removed from the Doctrine & Covenants as they reflect the Biblical view of the Godhead.

Christianity

The apostles and prophets of Biblical times teach that God is a spirit, invisible, transcending the universe having no physical boundaries.

> God is spirit, and those who worship Him must worship in spirit and truth.
> — *John 4:24*

> Where can I go from Your Spirit? Or where can I flee from Your presence? If I ascend to heaven, You are there; If I make my bed in Sheol, behold, You are there.
> — *Psalm 139:7-8*

> ... "Do I not fill the heavens and the earth?" declares the LORD.
> — *Jeremiah 23:24*

> ... Behold, heaven and the highest heaven cannot contain You...
> — *1 Kings 8:27, 2 Chronicles 6:18*

... the heavens and the highest heavens cannot contain Him...
— *2 Chronicles 2:6*

Now to the King eternal, immortal, invisible, the only God...
— *1 Timothy 1:17*

Who is the image of the invisible God...
— *Colossians 1:15*

Polytheism

Mormonism teaches Polytheism: the belief in multiple gods.

- The Godhead is comprised of three gods
- Heavenly Father has a father, and so on
- God the father is married to Heavenly Mother(s)
- There are other gods beyond the Godhead
- Mormons may become a God

The Trinity is comprised of three gods

Mormonism teaches that Heavenly Father, Jesus Christ, and the Holy Ghost are three separate and distinct gods united in purpose over our planet. This cooperation is called the Godhead.

> I will preach on the plurality of Gods... I have always declared God to be a distinct personage, Jesus Christ a separate and distinct personage from God the Father, and that the Holy Ghost was a distinct personage and a Spirit: and these three constitute three distinct personages and three Gods.
> — Joseph Smith, Mormonism founder, *History of the Church 6:474*

God the Father has a father

General Authorities teach that Heavenly Father has a father.

> We shall go back to our Father and God, who is connected with one who is still farther back; and this Father is connected with one still further back, and so on.
> — Heber C. Kimball, First Presidency Counselor, *Journal of Discourses 5:19*

> God is an exalted man... The Prophet taught that our Father had a Father and so on.
> — Joseph Fielding Smith, Mormon prophet, *Doctrines of Salvation, 1:10,12*

God is a natural man... Where did he get his knowledge from? From his Father, just as we get knowledge from our earthly parents.
— Heber C. Kimball, First Presidency Counselor, *Journal of Discourses 8:211*

God the Father is married to Heavenly Mother(s)
The Mormon church teaches that Heavenly Father is married. The teaching of a Heavenly Mother permeates LDS thought today.

Sex Among the Gods. Since we have a Father who is our God, we must also have a mother, who possesses the attributes of Godhood.
— John A. Widstoe, Mormon apostle, *Rational Theology, p.64-65*

Man, as a spirit, was begotten and born of Heavenly Parents.
— Joseph F. Smith, Mormon prophet, *Improvement Era 13:80*

The stupendous truth of the existence of a Heavenly Mother, as well as a Heavenly Father, became established facts in Mormon theology.
— Milton R. Hunter, Mormon Seventy, *The Gospel Throughout The Ages, p.99*

Implicit in the Christian verity that all men are the spirit children of an Eternal Father is the usually unspoken truth that they are also the offspring of an Eternal Mother.
— Bruce R. McConkie, Mormon apostle, *Mormon Doctrine, p.516 (1966)*

Other gods
General Authorities teach that there are many gods beyond the LDS Godhead.

I will preach on the plurality of Gods (p.474)... The heads of the Gods appointed one God for us (p.476)...
— Joseph Smith, Mormonism founder, *History of the Church 6:474*

A Council of the Gods. In the beginning, the head of the Gods called a council of the Gods; and they came together and concocted a plan to create the world and people it.
— Joseph Smith, Mormonism founder, *Ensign, April 1971, p.13-14*

If we should take a million of worlds like this and number their particles, we should find that there are more Gods than there are particles of matter in those worlds... One world has a personal God or Father, and the inhabitants thereof worship the attributes of that God, another world has another, and they worship His attributes...
— Orson Pratt, Mormon apostle, *Journal of Discourses 2:345*

How many Gods there are, I do not know. But there never was a time when there were not Gods and worlds, and when men were not passing through the same ordeals that we are now passing through.
— Brigham Young, Mormon prophet, *Journal of Discourses 7:333*

God, angel and similar terms denote merely intelligent beings of varying degree of development. The thought, however, that there is a plurality of gods and other beings of varying grades, is a though of fundamental truth.
— John A. Widstoe, Mormon apostle, *Rational Theology, p.62*

Consequently every earth has its redeemer, and every earth has its tempter; and every earth, and the people thereof, in their turn and time, receive all that we receive, and pass through all the ordeals that we are passing through.
— Brigham Young, Mormon prophet, *Journal of Discourses 14:71-72*

But if God the Father was not always God, but came to his present exalted position by degrees of progress as indicated in the teachings of the prophet, how has there been a

God from all eternity? The answer is that there has been and there now exists an endless line of Gods, stretching back into the eternities, that had no beginning and will have no end. Their existence runs parallel with endless duration, and their dominions are as limitless as boundless space.

— B. H. Roberts, LDS church historian, *A New Witnesses for God 1:476*

Evolving Doctrine

Skeptics claim that Joseph Smith's views evolved from monotheism to polytheism. Joseph's earliest works and statements (including the Book of Mormon and the Inspired Version) reflect Monotheism.

- In 1833, when Joseph rewrote Genesis (Book of Moses), he reinforced monotheism. In 1842 when he rewrote Genesis (Book of Abraham) he reinforced polytheism.

Book of Moses, Chapter 2 (1833)	**Book of Abraham, Chapter 4 (1842)**
2 And the earth was without form, and void; and **I** caused darkness to come up upon the face of the deep; and **my Spirit** moved upon the face of the water; **for I am God,**	2 And the earth, after it was formed, was empty and desolate, because **they** had not formed anything but the earth; and darkness reigned upon the face of the deep, and **the Spirit of the Gods** was brooding upon the face of the waters.
3 And **I, God**, said: Let there be light; and there was light.	3 And **they (the Gods)** said: Let there be light; and there was light.
4 And **I, God**, saw the light; and that light was good. And **I, God**, divided the light from the darkness.	4 And **they (the Gods)** comprehended the light, for it was bright; and they divided the light, or caused it to be divided, from the darkness.
5 And **I, God**, called the light Day; and the darkness, **I** called Night; and this **I** did by the word of **my** power, and it was done as **I** spake; and the evening and the morning were the first day.	5 And **the Gods** called the light Day, and the darkness **they** called Night. And it came to pass that from the evening until morning **they** called night; and from the morning until the evening **they** called day; and this was the first, or the beginning, of that which **they** called day and night.

- Important theological changes were made in the book of Mormon to separate God the Father and Jesus Christ.

	1830 Original Edition	**Modern editions**
1 Nephi 11:18	And he said unto me: Behold, the virgin which thou seest is the mother of God after the manner of the flesh	And he said unto me: Behold, the virgin whom thou seest is the mother of **the Son of** God, after the manner of the flesh.
1 Nephi 11:21	And the angel said unto me: Behold the Lamb of God, yea, even the Eternal Father.	And the angel said unto me: Behold the Lamb of God, yea, even **the Son of** the Eternal Father!
1 Nephi 11:32	... And I looked and beheld the Lamb of God, that he was taken by the people, yea, the everlasting God was judged of the world.	... And I looked and beheld the Lamb of God, that he was taken by the people; yea, **the Son of** the everlasting God was judged of the world.
1 Nephi 13:40	...that the Lamb of God is the Eternal Father and the Savior of the world...	...that the Lamb of God is **the Son of** the Eternal Father, and the Savior of the world...

Christianity

The prophets and apostles of Biblical times taught that there is only One God.

> Then he said, "Tomorrow." So he said, "May it be according to your word, that you may know that there is no one like the LORD our God.
>
> — *Exodus 8:10*

> To you it was shown that you might know that the LORD, He is God; there is no other besides Him.
>
> — *Deuteronomy 4:35*

> Know therefore today, and take it to your heart, that the LORD, He is God in heaven above and on the earth below; there is no other.
>
> — *Deuteronomy 4:39*

Hear, O Israel! The LORD is our God, the LORD is one!
— *Deuteronomy 6:4, cf. Mark 12:29*

See now that I, I am He, and there is no god besides Me ...
— *Deuteronomy 32:39*

There is no one holy like the LORD, indeed, there is no one besides You, nor is there any rock like our God.
—*1 Samuel 2:2*

... O Lord GOD; for there is none like You, and there is no God besides You ...
— *2 Samuel 7:22*

O LORD, there is none like You, nor is there any God besides You...
— *1 Chronicles 17:20*

You alone are the LORD, You have made the heavens, the heaven of heavens with all their host...
— *Nehemiah 9:6*

... So that you may know and believe Me and understand that I am He, before Me there was no God formed, and there will be none after Me.
— *Isaiah 43:10*

Thus says the LORD, the King of Israel and his Redeemer, the LORD of hosts: 'I am the first and I am the last, and there is no God besides Me.'
— *Isaiah 44:6*

... Is there any God besides Me, Or is there any other Rock? I know of none.

— *Isaiah 44:8*

I am the LORD, and there is no other; Besides Me there is no God ...
— *Isaiah 45:5*

For thus says the LORD, who created the heavens (He is the God who formed the earth and made it, He established it and did not create it a waste place, but formed it to be inhabited), "I am the LORD, and there is none else."
— *Isaiah 45:18*

... And there is no other God besides Me, A righteous God and a Savior; There is none except Me. "Turn to Me and be saved, all the ends of the earth; For I am God, and there is no other.
— *Isaiah 45:21-22*

Remember the former things long past, For I am God, and there is no other; I am God, and there is no one like Me.
— *Isaiah 46:9*

There is none like You, O LORD; You are great, and great is Your name in might.
— *Jeremiah 10:6*

And the scribe said unto him, Well, Master, thou hast said the truth: for there is one God; and there is none other but he.
— *Mark 12:32 KJV*

Seeing it is one God, which shall justify the circumcision by faith, and uncircumcision through faith.
— *Romans 3:30 KJV*

Therefore concerning the eating of things sacrificed to idols, we know that there is no such thing as an idol in the world, and that there is no God but one.
— *I Corinthians 8:4*

Now a mediator is not for one party only; whereas God is only one.
— *Galatians 3:20*

You believe that God is one. You do well; the demons also believe, and shudder.
— *James 2:19*

The Book of Mormon does not teach the modern LDS doctrine but reflects Christian monotheism.

And Zeezrom said unto him:
Thou sayest there is a true and living God?
And Amulek said: Yea, there is a true and living God.
Now Zeezrom said: Is there more than one God?
And he answered, No.
— *Alma 11:26-29*

...See that ye remember these things; for he said there is but one God...
— *Alma 11:35*

And the people ... also testified that there was but one God ...
— *Alma 14:5*

And the honor be to the Father, and to the Son, and to the Holy Ghost, which is one God. Amen.
— *Testimony of Three Witnesses*

The Bible teaches that Jesus Christ is the One God manifest in the flesh.

> Great is the mystery of godliness: God was manifest in the flesh...
> — *1 Timothy 3:16*

> In Christ all the fullness of Deity dwells in bodily form...
> — *Colossians 2:9*

> God was in Christ reconciling the world to Himself...
> — *2 Corinthians 5:19*

> "He who has seen Me has seen the Father"
> — *John 14:9*

> There is one body and one Spirit, just as also you were called in one hope of your calling; one Lord, one faith, one baptism, one God and Father of all who is over all and through all and in all.
> — *Ephesians 4:4-6*

> Beware lest any man spoil you through philosophy and vain deceit, after the tradition of men, after the rudiments of the world, and not after Christ, for in Him dwelleth all the fulness of the Godhead bodily.
> — *Colossians 2:8-9*

> In the beginning was the Word, and the Word was with God, and the Word was God... And the Word became flesh, and dwelt among us.
> — *John 1:1,14*

The Kenosis—God emptied himself to become a man:

> Have this attitude in yourselves which was also in Christ Jesus, who, although He existed in the form of God, did not regard equality with God a thing to be grasped, but emptied Himself, taking the form of a bond-servant, and being made in the likeness of men. Being found in appearance as a man, He humbled Himself by becoming obedient to the point of death, even death on a cross.
> — *Philippians 2:5-8*

The Book of Mormon does not teach the modern LDS doctrine of three Gods, but teaches that God came down and became a man. God in the flesh is called the Son. God as flesh is subordinate to the Spirit, called the Father—two titles, one God.

> ... understand that God himself shall come down among the children of men, and shall redeem his people. And because he dwelleth in flesh he shall be called the Son of God, and having subjected the flesh to the will of the Father, being the Father and the Son—The Father, because he was conceived by the power of God; and the Son, because of the flesh; thus becoming the Father and Son—And they are one God, yea, the very Eternal Father of heaven and of earth. And thus the flesh becoming subject to the Spirit, or the Son to the Father, being one God ...
> — *Mosiah 15:1-5*

> ... And now, behold, this is the doctrine of Christ, and the only and true doctrine of the Father, and of the Son, and of the Holy Ghost, which is one God, without end. Amen.
> — *2 Nephi 31:21*

> ... unto the Father, and unto the Son, and unto the Holy Ghost, which are one God, in a state of happiness which hath no end.
> — *Mormon 7:7*

> ... Christ the Son, and God the Father, and the Holy Spirit, which is one Eternal God ...

— *Alma 11:44*

> For if there be no Christ there be no God; and if there be no God we are not, for there could have been no creation. But there is a God, and he is Christ, and he cometh in the fulness of his own time.
> — *2 Nephi 11:7*

Joseph Smith's translation (JST) of the Bible reinforces the Christian doctrine of the Trinity: One God manifest in three persons.

> For there are three that bear record in heaven, the Father, the Word, and the Holy Ghost; and these three are one.
> — *1 John 5:7 JST*

Part of the LDS canon for 86 years, the Lectures on Faith were removed from the Doctrine & Covenants in 1921 as they do not teach modern LDS polytheism.

> The Father being a personage of spirit... The Son, who was in the bosom of the Father, a personage of tabernacle, made or fashioned like unto man... is called the Son because of the flesh... possessing the same mind with the Father; which Mind is the Holy Spirit... and these three are one... and these three constitute the Godhead and are one: the Father and the Son possessing the same mind... the Spirit of the Father.
> — *Doctrine & Covenants: Lectures on Faith, V (removed 1921)*

The Book of Mormon says that Jesus Christ is the Father.

> ...Behold, I am Jesus Christ. I am the Father and the Son...
> — *Ether 3:14*

Now Zeezrom saith again unto him: Is the Son of God the very Eternal Father? And Amulek said unto him:

Yea, he is the very Eternal Father

— *Alma 11:38-39*

And they are one God, yea, the very Eternal Father of heaven and of earth.
— *Mosiah 15:4*

Joseph Smith's translation of the Bible says that Jesus is the Father.

... no man knoweth that the Son is the Father, and the Father is the Son, but him to whom the Son will reveal it ...
— *Luke 10:23 JST, cf. Luke 10:22*

Exaltation—Mormons may become Gods

"As man is God once was, as God is man may become."
— Mormon prophet Lorenzo Snow

Mormonism teaches that through obedience and loyalty to the LDS church, its faithful members can become Gods.

> Then shall they be gods, because they have no end; therefore shall they be from everlasting to everlasting, because they continue; then shall they be above all, because all things are subject unto them. Then shall they be gods, because they have all power, and the angels are subject unto them. Verily, verily, I say unto you, except ye abide my law ye cannot attain to this glory.
> — *Doctrine and Covenants 132:20-21*

> Here, then, is eternal life—to know the only wise and true God; and you have got to learn how to be gods yourselves, and to be kings and priests to God, the same as all gods have done before you, namely, by going from one small degree to another, and from a small capacity to a great one; from grace to grace, from exaltation to exaltation, until you attain to the resurrection of the dead, and are able to dwell in everlasting burnings, and to sit in glory, as do those who sit enthroned in everlasting power...
>
> What is it? To inherit the same power, the same glory and the same exaltation, until you arrive at the station of a god, and ascend the throne of eternal power, the same as those who have gone before.
> — Joseph Smith, Mormonism founder, *King Follett Sermon, Ensign, April 1971*

Kolob

Mormon authorities and scripture teach that God resides near a planet or star named Kolob.

And I saw the stars, that they were very great, and that one of them was nearest unto the throne of God; and there were many great ones which were near unto it; And the Lord said unto me: These are the governing ones; and the name of the great one is Kolob, because it is near unto me, for I am the Lord thy God: I have set this one to govern all those which belong to the same order as that upon which thou standest.
— *Book of Abraham 3:2-3*

Kolob, signifying the first creation, nearest to the celestial, or the residence of God.
— *Book of Abraham, Facsimile 2, Figure 1*

Enish-go-on-dosh a governing planet—the Sun.
— *Book of Abraham, Facsimile 2, Figure 5*
(Note: planet and star are used interchangeably)

Kolob... signifies the first great grand governing fixed star which is the farthest that ever has been discovered by the fathers which was discovered by Methusela and also by Abraham.
— Joseph Smith, Mormon prophet, *Kirtland Egyptian Papers, Grammar p.34*

In this passage will be found the germ of that system of the construction and movement of planetary systems that make up the universe, set forth in the teachings of Joseph Smith. Here it may be seen that there are many great stars—the "governing ones," near together, and from among them rises one pre-eminent in greatness—Kolob—which governs all the rest that are of the same order as that to which our solar system belongs."
— B. H. Roberts, LDS church historian, *A New Witness for God, p. 447*

Kolob... the planet nearest unto the habitation of the Eternal Father.
— Brigham Young, Mormon prophet, *Ensign, November 1971*

Thou longed, thou sighed and thou prayed to thy Father in heaven for the time to arrive when thou couldst come to this earth, which had fled and fallen from where it was first organised, near the planet Kolob.
— John Taylor, Mormon prophet, *Liahona, the Elder's Journal, Vol. 5, No. 38, March 7, 1908*

Adam God Doctrine

Mormonism's second and longest serving prophet, Brigham Young, publicly taught that Adam is God. Brigham said he learned this doctrine from Joseph Smith. If true, then three of the earliest Mormon prophets believed that Adam is God.

Sources

Quotes in chronological order

> When our father Adam came into the garden of Eden, he came into it with a celestial body, and brought Eve, one of his wives, with him. He helped to make and organize this world. He is MICHAEL, the Archangel, the ANCIENT OF DAYS! about whom holy men have written and spoken – HE is our FATHER and our GOD, and the only God with whom WE have to do. Every man upon the earth, professing Christian or non-professing, must hear it, and will know it sooner or later... When the Virgin Mary conceived the child Jesus, the Father had begotten him in his own likeness. He was not begotten by the Holy Ghost. And who is the Father? He is the first of the human family...
>
> [p.51] Jesus, our elder brother, was begotten in the flesh by the same character that was in the garden of Eden, and who is our Father in Heaven. Now, let all who may hear these doctrines, pause before they make light of them, or treat them with indifference, for they will prove their salvation or damnation.
> — Brigham Young, Mormon prophet, *April 9, 1852, 22nd Annual General Conference, Journal of Discourses 1:50-51*

> Another meeting this evening. President B. Young taught that Adam was the Father of Jesus and the only God to us.
> — Hosea Stout, Seventies president, *Diary 2:435 - April 9, 1852*

Our Father begat all the spirits that were before any tabernacles were made. When our Father came into the Garden he came with his celestial body and brought one of his wives with him and ate of the fruit of the garden until he could begat a tabernacle. And Adam is Michael or God and all the God that we have any thing to do with.
— Wilford Woodruff, Mormon prophet, *Diary - April 9, 1852*

Jesus Christ was his God and the God and Father of Jesus Christ was Adam.
— Heber C. Kimball, First Presidency Counselor, *April 10, 1852, 22nd Annual General Conference*

After men have got their exaltations and their crowns — have become Gods, even the sons of God — are made Kings of kings and Lords of lords, they have the power then of propagating their species in spirit; and that is the first of their operations with regard to organizing a world. Power is then given to them to organize the elements, and then commence the organization of tabernacles. How can they do it? Have they to go to that earth? Yes, an Adam will have to go there, and he cannot do without Eve; he must have Eve to commence the work of generation, and they will go into the garden, and continue to eat and drink of the fruits of the corporeal world, until this greater matter is diffused sufficiently through their celestial bodies to enable them, according to the established laws, to produce mortal tabernacles for their spiritual children.
— Brigham Young, Mormon prophet, *August 28, 1852, Journal of Discourses 6:275*
Note: Modern LDS doctrine teaches that Heavenly Father is the parent of spiritual babies before they obtain physical bodies through human reproduction. Here, Brigham teaches that Adam and Eve are both the parents of the spiritual babies as well as their physical bodies.

Our Father Adam.—The extract from the Journal of Discourses may startle some of our readers, but we would wish them to recollect that in this last dispensation God will send forth, by His servants, things new as well as old, until man is perfected in the truth. And we would here take occasion to remark, that it would be well if all our readers would

secure a copy of the Journal of Discourses as it is issued, and also of every standard work of the Church; and not only secure these works, but attentively read them, and thoroughly study the principles they contain. Those of the Saints who fail to obtain the standard publications of the Church, will not be likely to prove very intelligent Saints, and will be very liable to wake up some day, and find themselves wonderfully behind the times, and consequently will not be able to stand the day of trial, which will come upon all the world. Without the intelligence that comes through the Holy Priesthood, the Saints cannot gain salvation, and this intelligence is given in the various publications of the Church. Who then will endanger his salvation by being behind the times? Not the wise, certainly.
— *Millennial Star 15:780, November 26, 1853*

President Young followed and made many good remarks... He said that our God was Father Adam. He was the Father of the Savior Jesus Christ, our God was no more or less than ADAM, Michael the Archangel.
— Wilford Woodruff, Mormon prophet, *Diary - February 19, 1854*

Concerning the item of doctrine... that Adam is our Father and God... the Prophet and Apostle Brigham has declared it, and that is the word of the Lord.
— Franklin D. Richards, Mormon apostle, *August 26, 1854, Millennial Star 16:534*

Elohim looked around upon the eternity of matter, and said to his associates, and those that he was pleased to call upon at that time for his counselors, with regard to the elements, worlds, planets, kingdoms and thrones; said he, "Yahovah Michael, see that eternal matter on all sides, this way and that way; we have already created worlds upon worlds, shall we create another world? Yes, go and organize the elements yonder in space;"... "Yahovah Michael, go and create a world, make it, organize it, form it; and then put upon it every thing in all the variety that you have seen... " Yahovah Michael, goes and does as he is told. What I am going to tell you, will no doubt astonish the whole of you. When Yahovah Michael had organized the world... Michael, or Adam, goes down to the new made world, and there he stays... Moses said Adam was made of the dust of the ground, but he did not say of what ground. I say he was not made of the dust of the ground of this earth, but he was made of the dust of the earth where he lived, where he honored his calling, believing in his Savior, or Elder Brother, and by his faithfulness, was redeemed, and got a glorious resurrection… Adam is the Father of our spirits… Now, many inquiries will be made about the Savior such as, "Who is he?" "Is he the Father of Adam?" "Is he the God of Adam?" When Christ has finished his labor and presented it to his father, then he, Adam will receive a fullness… Adam then, was a resurrected being; and I reckon, our spirits and the spirits of all the human family were begotten by Adam, and born of Eve. "How are we going to know this?" I reckon it… I tell you, when you see your Father in the heavens, you will see Adam; when you see your Mother that bears your spirit, you will see mother Eve...

— Brigham Young, Mormon prophet, *October 8, 1854, 24th Semiannual General Conference*

I have learned by experience that there is but one God that pertains to this people, and He is the God that pertains to this earth – the first man. That first man sent his own Son to redeem the word...

— Heber C. Kimball, First Presidency Counselor, *June 29, 1856, Journal of Discourses 4:1*

We believe in our God the great Prince of His race,

The Archangel Michael, the Ancient of Days,

Our own Father Adam, earth's Lord, as is plain,

Who'll counsel and fight for his children again.

We believe in His Son, Jesus Christ...

— Franklin D. Richards, Mormon apostle, *Sacred Hymns and Spiritual Songs for the Church of Jesus Christ of Latter-day Saints, p. 375, 1856 - 11th Edition*

President Young said Adam was Michael the Archangel, & he was the Father of Jesus Christ & was our God & that Joseph taught this principle.
— Wilford Woodruff, Mormon prophet, *Diary - December 16, 1867*

It was Joseph's doctrine that Adam was God... God comes to earth and eats and partakes of fruit. Joseph could not reveal what was revealed to him, and if Joseph had it revealed, he was not told to reveal it.
— *Quorum of Twelve meeting minutes, April 4, 1860*

Some years ago, I advanced a doctrine with regard to Adam being our father and God, that will be a curse to many of the Elders of Israel because of their folly. With regard to it they yet grovel in darkness and will. It is one of the most glorious revealments of the economy of heaven, yet the world hold derision. Had I revealed the doctrine of baptism from the dead instead of Joseph Smith there are men around me who would have ridiculed the idea until dooms day. But they are ignorant and stupid like the dumb ass.
— Brigham Young, Mormon prophet, *October 8, 1861, Manuscript Address*

How much unbelief exists in the minds of the Latter-day Saints in regard to one particular doctrine which I revealed to them, and which God revealed to me — namely that Adam is our Father and God.
— Brigham Young, Mormon prophet, *Deseret News - June 18, 1873*

We have heard a great deal about Adam and Eve. how they were formed... he was made of the dust of the earth but not of this earth... he was made just the same way you and I are made but on another earth. Adam was an immortal being when he came. on this earth he had lived on an earth similar to ours... and had begotten all the spirit that was to come to this earth. and Eve our common Mother who is the mother of all living bore those spirits in the celestial world... Father Adam's oldest son (Jesus the Saviour) who is the heir of the family is Father Adams first begotten in the spirit World. who according to the flesh is the only begotten as it is written. In his divinity he having gone back into the

spirit World. and came in the spirit to Mary and she conceived for when Adam and Eve got through with their Work on this earth. they did not lay their bodies down in the dust, but returned to the spirit world from whence they came.
— L. John Nuttall, Brigham Young's personal secretary, *Diary - February 7, 1877*

Adam is our father and God and no use to discuss it with Josephites or any one else.
— Wilford Woodruff, Mormon prophet, *Brigham Young Jr.'s Journal - April 4, 1897*
Note: At the time of this statement (nearly 45 years after Young's 1852 General Conference address), Woodruff has been the LDS church President for eight years.

Consequences

- Who God is does not change on the whim of a Mormon prophet. God cannot be Adam one day and someone else another day.
- False prophets teach or believe things contrary to the truth of God.
- For Mormons the implications are eternal: is Adam God?

Yes	No
The LDS church is now led by false prophets who deny this doctrine.	The LDS church's second and longest serving prophet was a false prophet.

Polygamy

Joseph Smith, founder of Mormonism, was the first Mormon prophet to practice polygamy.

- He took as many as 48 wives.
- Many were teenagers, as young as 13 years old.
- Many were already married to other men and continued in polyandry—having more than one husband.
- He married pairs of sisters, and even took a mother and her daughter for wives.

The wives of the prophets

The first seven Mormon prophets had at least 135 wives.

Mormon prophet	Number of wives
Joseph Smith	48
Brigham Young	55
John Taylor	7
Wilford Woodruff	5
Lorenzo Snow	11
Joseph F. Smith	6
Heber J. Grant	3

Summary of Events

- From 1830 to 1876, LDS scripture was consistent in prohibited polygamy: Book of Mormon: Jacob, chapter 2; Doctrine and Covenants, Section 101 (removed in 1876).
- During this time the church publicly taught against polygamy and denied practicing it, while church authorities were privately taking plural wives.

- In 1852 Brigham Young, the second Mormon prophet, publicly admitted the practice of polygamy.
- In 1876, Section 132 of the Doctrine and Covenants, which allows polygamy, was added to the Doctrine and Covenants. Section 101 which condemns it was removed. Section 132 remains part of the LDS canon today.
- Under pressure from the federal government to end polygamy, which passed law to disincorporate the church and seize its assets, Wilford Woodruff, the fourth Mormon prophet, announced he had received a "revelation" to officially end the practice. This announcement is knows as the 1890 Manifesto or Official Declaration—1.
- 14 years later, congressional hearings uncover church authorities still taking plural wives in secret, in disregard to the 1890 revelation. In response, Joseph F. Smith, the sixth Mormon prophet, issued what is known as the "Second Manifesto" condemning polygamy.
- As late as 1943 it was uncovered that Mormon apostle Richard Lyman was secretly practicing polygamy.

Timeline

1827	Joseph Smith marries Emma Hale
1830	**Original Book of Mormon published and condemns polygamy** But the word of God burdens me because of your grosser crimes. For behold thus saith the Lord: This people begin to wax in iniquity; they understand not the scriptures for they seek to excuse themselves in committing whoredoms because of the things which were written concerning David and Solomon his son. Behold David and Solomon truly had many wives and concubines which thing was abominable before me saith the Lord... Wherefore my brethren hear me and hearken to the word of the Lord: For there shall not any man among you have save it be one wife; and concubines he shall have none. — *Book of Mormon, Jacob 2:23-24, 27*
1833	Joseph Smith marries Fanny Alger

August, 1835	Official LDS publication denies polygamy charges Inasmuch as this Church of Christ has been reproached with the crime of fornication and polygamy we declare that we believe that one man should have one wife and one woman but one husband. — *Messenger and Advocate 1:163, History of the Church 2:247*
1835-1876	**Doctrines and Covenants published with Section 101 condemning polygamy** ON MARRIAGE. Inasmuch as this church of Christ has been reproached with the crime of fornication, and polygamy: we declare that we believe, that one man should have one wife; and one woman, but one husband... We have given the above rule of marriage as the only one practiced in this church... We the undersigned members of the church of Jesus Christ of Latter-Day Saints and residents of the city of Nauvoo, persons of families do hereby certify and declare that we know of no other rule or system of marriage than the one published from the Book of Doctrine and Covenants... We the undersigned members of the ladies' relief society, and married females do certify and declare that we know of no system of marriage being practiced in the church of Jesus Christ of Latter Day Saints save the one contained in the Book of Doctrine and Covenants... — *Doctrine and Covenants, Section 101 (1835-1876)*
April, 1837	General Authorities issue statement condemning polygamy 1st-That we will have no fellowship whatever with any Elder belonging to the quorums of the Seventies who is guilty of polygamy or any offense of the kind, and who does not in all things conform to the laws of the church contained in the Bible and in the Book of Doctrine and Covenants. — *Quorum of Seventies Resolution #1, Messenger and Advocate 3:511*
1838	Joseph Smith marries Lucinda Harris, who was at the time married to George Harris.
January, 1838	Oliver Cowdery confronts Joseph Smith about his polygamy When he [Joseph Smith] was there we had some conversation in which in every instance I did not fail to affirm that what I had said was strictly true. A dirty, nasty, filthy affair of his and Fanny Alger's was talked over in which I strictly declared that I had never deviated from the truth in the matter, and as I supposed was admitted by himself.

	— Oliver Cowdery, Assistant President and Book of Mormon witness, *Letter recorded by his brother Warren Cowdery, Photograph available in The Mormon Kingdom, vol. 1, p.27*
April, 1838	Oliver Cowdery is excommunicated.
July, 1838	Joseph Smith denies polygamy Question 7th. Do the Mormons believe in having more wives than one? Answer. No, not at the same time. — Joseph Smith, Mormonism founder, *Elder's Journal, p.43*
December, 1838	Joseph Smith denies polygamy We have heard that it is reported by some, that some of us should have said, that we not only dedicated our property, but our families also to the Lord; and Satan, taking advantage of this, has perverted it into licentiousness, such as a community of wives, which is an abomination in the sight of God. — Joseph Smith, Mormonism founder, *Teachings of the Prophet Joseph Smith, p.127, History of the Church 3:230*
April, 1841	Joseph Smith marries Louise Beaman
October, 1841	Joseph Smith marries Zina Jacobs, who at the time was married to Henry Jacobs
December, 1841	Joseph Smith marries Presendia Buell
1842	Joseph Smith marries Sally Fuller and Sarah Bapson.
January 6, 1842	Joseph Smith marries Agnes Coolbrith, who was the widow of Don Carlos (Joseph's brother)
January 17, 1842	Joseph Smith marries Mary Lightner, who at the time was married to Adam Lightner
February, 1842	Joseph Smith marries Sylvia Lyon, who at the time was married to Windsor Lyon. Joseph would also marry Sylvia's mother Patty the next month.
March 1, 1842	**12 Article of Faith** Joseph Smith pens the 12th Article of Faith. Polygamy was a violation of the law. We believe in being subject to kings, presidents, rulers, and magistrates, in obeying, honoring, and sustaining the law. — Joseph Smith, Mormonism founder, *Wentworth Letter*

March 9, 1842	Joseph Smith marries Patty Sessions, who at the time was married to David Sessions. Joseph married Patty's daughter Sylvia the previous month.
April, 1842	Joseph Smith marries Marinda Hyde, who at the time was married to Orson Hyde.
June, 1842	Joseph Smith marries Sarah Cleveland; Eliza Snow; and Elizabeth Durfee, who at the time was married to Jabez Durfee.
July, 1842	Joseph Smith marries Delcena Sherman and Sarah Whitney.
August, 1842	Official LDS church publication denies polygamy But for the information of those who might be assailed by those foolish tales about two wives we would say that no such principle ever existed among the Latter-Day Saints and ever will; this is well known to all who are acquainted with our books and actions. — *Millennial Star, Vol. 3, No. 4, p.73* **Joseph Smith marries Martha McBride**
September, 1842	Official LDS publication denies polygamy Inasmuch as the public mind has been unjustly abused... we make an extract on the subject of marriage, showing the rule of the church on this important matter. The extract is from the Book of Doctrine and Covenants, and is the only rule allowed by the church. "All legal contracts of marriage made before a person is baptized into this church, should be held sacred and fulfilled. Inasmuch as this church of Christ has been reproached with the crime of fornication, and polygamy: we declare that we believe, that one man should have one wife; and one woman." — *Times and Seasons 4:909*
October, 1842	Official LDS publication reprints D&C 101 prohibiting polygamy ...Inasmuch as this church of Christ has been reproached with the crime of fornication, and polygamy: we declare that we believe, that one man should have one wife; and one woman, but one husband... — *Times and Seasons 3:939-940*
1843	Joseph Smith marries Hanna Ells and 14 year old Nancy Winchester
February, 1843	Joseph Smith marries Ruth Sayers
March, 1843	Joseph Smith marries Emily Partridge

April, 1843	Joseph Smith marries Almera Johnson
May, 1843	Joseph Smith marries Lucy Walker, 14 year old Helen Kimball, and sisters Sarah and Maria Lawrence
Spring, 1843	Joseph Smith marries 16 year old Flora Woodworth
June, 1843	Joseph Smith marries Elvira Holmes and Rhoda Richards
July, 1843	**"Revelation" on Plurality of Wives (Doctrine and Covenants, Section 132)** • Joseph Smith dictates a "revelation" requiring the practice of polygamy to obtain exaltation—becoming gods (v.1-6, 20). • This revelation would not be canonized until 1876 as Section 132 of the Doctrine and Covenants. It remains part of the LDS canon today. • Up until now Joseph hid his marital trysts from his first wife Emma. • Joseph's brother Hyrum attempted to present this "divine revelation" to win Emma's approval of her husband's behavior. Emma rejected it. • The revelation specifically states that if Emma rejects it she would be destroyed (v.54, 64). That did not happen, however it was Joseph who died within a year from now. Emma, who was 39 years at this time lived to be 75. • Note that additional wives were to be virgins (v.61-62). By taking wives who were already married Joseph did not even follow his own revelation! • For additional information see History of the Church 5:501-508
January, 1844	Despite the July revelation requiring polygamy, the Mormon church continued to deny it Inasmuch as this church of Christ has been reproached with the crime of fornication and polygamy, we declare that we believe, that one man should have but one wife, and one woman but one husband... We wish these doctrines to be taught by all that are in the ministry, that the people may know our faith respecting them, and also to correct the public mind in respect to the church. — *Millennial Star, Vol. 4, No. 9, p.144*
February, 1844	Joseph Smith condemns the practice of polygamy As we have lately been credibly informed, that an Elder of the Church of Jesus Christ, of Latter-day Saints, by the name of Hyram Brown, has been preaching polygamy, and other false and corrupt doctrines, in the county of Lapeer, state of Michigan. This is to notify him and the Church in general, that he has been cut off from the church, for his iniquity. — Joseph Smith, Mormonism founder, *Times and Seasons 5:423*

April, 1844	Joseph Smith denies polygamy We very frequently receive letters from elders and individuals abroad, inquiring of us whether certain statements that they hear, and have written to them, are true: some pertaining to John C. Bennet's spiritual wife system; others in regard to immoral conduct, practiced by individuals, and sanctioned by the church; and as it is impossible for us to answer all of them, we take this opportunity of answering them all, once for all. In the first place, we cannot but express our surprise that any elder or priest who has been in Nauvoo, and has had an opportunity of hearing the principles of truth advanced, should for one moment give credence to the idea that anything like iniquity is practiced, much less taught or sanctioned, by the authorities of the Church of Jesus Christ of Latter Day Saints. If any man writes to you, or preaches to you, doctrines contrary to the Bible, the Book of Mormon, or the book of Doctrine and Covenants, set him down as an imposter. — Joseph Smith, Mormonism founder, *Times and Seasons, Vol.5, No.7, p.491*
March, 1844	Under the direction of Joseph Smith, Hyrum Smith officiated a polygamous wedding for Mormon apostle Erastus Snow. Testimony of Erastus Snow, Mormon apostle, The Historical Record 6:232
March 15, 1844	Joseph's brother Hyrum Smith denies polygamy Whereas brother Richard Hewitt has called on me to-day, to know my views concerning some doctrines that are preached in your place, and states to me that some of your elders say, that a man having a certain priesthood, may have as many wives as he pleases, and that doctrine is taught here: I say unto you that that man teaches false doctrine, for there is no such doctrine taught here. And any man that is found teaching privately or publicly any such doctrine, is culpable, and will stand a chance to be brought before the High Council, and loose his license and membership also: therefore he had better beware what he is about. — Hyrum Smith, Assistant President, *Times and Seasons 5:474*
April, 1844	**Fallout: Presidency Counselors** After Jane Law rebuffs Joseph Smith's proposal to marry him, her husband William Law, who was Joseph's *Second Counselor of the First Presidency* is excommunicated. Austin Cowles, *First Counselor*, quits the church in protest.
May, 1844	Joseph Smith denies polygamy I had not been married scarcely five minutes, and made on proclamation of the Gospel, before it was reported that I had seven wives. This new holy prophet [William Law] has gone to Carthage and swore that I had told him that I was

	guilty of adultery. This spiritual wifeism! Why, a man dares not speak or wink, for fear of being accused of this... What a thing it is for a man to be accused of committing adultery, and having seven wives, when I can only find one. I am the same man, and as innocent as I was fourteen years ago. — Joseph Smith, Mormonism founder, *History of the Church 6:410-411*
June 7, 1844	Excommunicated Second Counselor William Law publishes a newspaper, the *Nauvoo Expositor*, containing testimony condemning Joseph's polygamy. It included testimony from former First Counselor Austin Coles. Forasmuch as the public mind hath been much agitated by a course of procedure in the Church of Jesus Christ of Latter Day Saints... In the latter part of the summer, 1843, the Patriarch, Hyrum Smith, did in the High Council, of which I was a member, introduce what he said was a revelation given through the Prophet... according to his reading there was contained the following doctrines... the doctrine of a plurality of wives, or marrying virgins; that "David and Solomon had many wives, yet in this they sinned not save in the matter of Uriah. This revelation with other evidence, that the aforesaid heresies were taught and practiced in the Church; determined me to leave the office of first counselor to the president of the Church at Nauvoo. — Austin Cowles, former First Counselor, *Nauvoo Expositor, Vol. 1, No. 1, p.2*
June 10, 1844	Joseph Smith, who is also the mayor of Nauvoo, orders the printing press of the *Nauvoo Expositor* destroyed. The Governor of Illinois has Joseph put in jail.
June 27, 1844	**Joseph Smith's death** An angry mob storms Joseph's cell and murders him.
October, 1844	Sidney Rigdon admits church authorities practice polygamy It is a fact, so well known, that the Twelve and their adherents have endeavored to carry this spiritual wife business in secret... and have gone to the most shameful and desperate lengths, to keep it from the public... I could bring facts which can be established in any court of justice, in relation to these vile abominations practiced under the garb of religion that would make humanity blush. — Sidney Rigdon, First Presidency Counselor, *Messenger and Advocate, Vol. 1, No. 1*
November, 1844	Official LDS publication denies polygamy The law of the land and the rules of the church do not allow one man to have more than one wife alive at once. — *Times and Seasons, Vol. 5, No. 21, p.715*

May, 1845	Official LDS publication denies polygamy. The Latter-day Saints are charged by their enemies, with the blackest crimes. Treason, murder, theft, polygamy, and adultery, are among the many crimes laid to their charge... As to the charge of polygamy, I will quote from the Book of Doctrine and Covenants, which is the subscribed faith of the church and is strictly enforced. Article Marriage, sec. 91, par. 4, says, "Inasmuch as this church of Christ has been reproached with the crime of fornication and polygamy, we declare that we believe that one man should have BUT ONE WIFE, and one woman but one husband." — *Times and Seasons 6:894*
1850	Mormon apostle John Taylor (the third Mormon prophet) publicly denies polygamy while at the time he is married to 7-12 wives. We are accused here of polygamy, and actions the most indelicate, obscene, and disgusting, such that none but a corrupt and depraved heart could have contrived. These things are too outrageous to admit of belief... I shall content myself by reading our views of chastity and marriage, from a work published by us, containing some of the articles of our Faith. "Doctrine and Covenants," [Cites D&C 101]. — John Taylor, Mormon prophet, *Three Nights' Public Discussion, p.8*
September 14, 1852	**Public Acknowledgement of Polygamy** In a special conference, the LDS church publicly acknowledges the practice of polygamy. Deseret News Extra, September 14, 1852
February, 1854	Mormon authority encourages polyandry When the family organization was revealed from heaven - the patriarchal order of God, and Joseph began, on the right and on the left, to add to his family, what a quaking there was in Israel. Says one brother to another, 'Joseph says all covenants are done away, and none are binding but the new covenants: now suppose Joseph should come and say he wanted your wife, what would you say to that?' 'I would tell him to go to hell.' This was the spirit of many in the early days of this Church... What would a man of God say, who felt aright, when Joseph asked him for his money? He would say, "Yes, and I wish I had more to help to build up the kingdom of God." Or if he came and said, "I want your wife?" "O yes," he would say, "here she is, there are plenty more"... Did the Prophet Joseph want every man's wife he asked for?... If such a man of God should come to me and say, "I want your gold and silver, or your wives," I should say, "Here they are, I wish I had more to give you, take all I have got." — Jedediah M. Grant, First Presidency Counselor, *Journal of Discourses 2:13-14*

July, 1857	Official LDS publication condemns polygamy before 1843 > The Latter-day Saints, from the rise of the Church in 1830, till the year 1843, had no authority to marry more than one wife each. To have done otherwise, would have been a great transgression. > — *Millennial Star, Vol. 19, No. 30, p.475*
1862	**Morrill Anti-Bigamy Act** United States President Abraham Lincoln signs the Morrill Anti-Bigamy Act targeting the LDS church.
August, 1866	Mormon prophet Brigham Young declares polygamy a priority over obtaining statehood for Utah. > "Do you think that we shall ever be admitted as a State into the Union without denying the principle of polygamy?" If we are not admitted until, we shall never be admitted. > — Brigham Young, Mormon prophet, *Journal of Discourses 11:269*
1876	**Doctrine and Covenants: Section 101 removed - Section 132 inserted** After 41 years as part of the LDS canon, Section 101 condemning polygamy is removed from the Doctrine and Covenants. Section 132 requiring polygamy for exaltation is canonized. Section 132 remains part of the canon today.
October, 1879	Mormon prophet John Taylor declares polygamy superior than obeying federal law. > I was asked, "Do you believe in obeying the laws of the United States?" Yes I do, in all except one—in fact I had not broken that. "What law is that?" The law in relation to polygamy. > — John Taylor, Mormon prophet, *Journal of Discourses 20:317*
February 19, 1887	**Edmunds-Tucker Act** The United States Congress passes the Edmunds-Tucker Act which permits the government to seize assets and disincorporate the LDS church for continuing to practice polygamy. The bill is enacted into law March 3.
May, 1887	Andrew Jenson, assistant LDS church historian, compiles what is considered the first list of wives of Joseph Smith. He documented 28 not including Emma. The Historical Record 6:233-234
October, 1890	**The 1890 Manifesto: Official Declaration—1** Under increasing pressure from the federal government, the sitting Mormon prophet, Wilford Wilson, issued a statement denying the practice of polygamy

	The Utah Commission, in their recent report to the Secretary of the Interior, allege that plural marriages are still being solemnized... also that in public discourses the leaders of the Church have taught, encouraged and urged the continuance of the practice of polygamy—I, therefore, as President of the Church of Jesus Christ of Latter-day Saints, do hereby, in the most solemn manner, declare that these charges are false. We are not teaching polygamy or plural marriage, nor permitting any person to enter into its practice. — Wilford Woodruff, Mormon prophet, *Doctrine and Covenants, Official Declaration—1* *Note: About a year later Wilford began referring to the statement as a "revelation". It was canonized in 1908.*
1892	Mormon prophet Lorenzo Snow condemns the practice of polygamy before 1843 Up to the time of the presentation of that revelation to the church and its acceptance by the church, the law of the church on marriage was the same as you have read, and which I referred to in the 1835 edition of the Book of Doctrine and Covenants, Exhibit E [D&C 101]. That was the law of the church up to the time of the purported revelation and its acceptance by the church; yes, sir, that is true. And a man that violated this law in the Book of Doctrine and Covenants, 1835 edition, until the acceptance of that revelation by the church, violated the law of the church if he practiced plural marriage. Yes, sir, he would have been cut off from the church. I think I should have been if I had. Before the giving of that revelation in 1843 if a man married more wives than one who were living at the same time, he would have been cut off from the church. It would have been adultery under the laws of the church and under the laws of the State, too. — Lorenzo Snow, Mormon prophet, *The Temple Lot Case, pp.320-322*
1904	**Reed Smoot Hearings** Hearings held by the United States Congress reveal that polygamy was still being practiced secretly among LDS church general authorities.
April, 1904	**Second Manifesto** In response to the Reed Smoot Hearings, Mormon prophet Joseph F. Smith issued yet another statement denying polygamy. Inasmuch as there are numerous reports in circulation that plural marriages have been entered into, contrary to the official declaration of President Woodruff of September 24, 1890, commonly called the manifesto, which was issued by President Woodruff, and adopted by the Church at its general conference, October 6, 1890, which forbade any marriages violative of the law of the land, I, Joseph F. Smith, President of the Church of Jesus Christ of Latter-day Saints,

	hereby affirm and declare that no such marriages have been solemnized with the sanction, consent, or knowledge of the Church of Jesus Christ of Latter-day Saints. And I hereby announce that all such marriages are prohibited, and if any officer or member of the Church shall assume to solemnize or enter into any such marriage, he will be deemed in transgression against the Church, and will be liable to be dealt with according to the rules and regulations thereof and excommunicated therefrom. — Joseph F. Smith, Mormon prophet, *Conference Report, p.97*
October, 1905	In protest, two Mormon apostles, John W. Taylor and Matthias F. Cowley resign from the Quorum of Twelve, as both continued to take plural wives.
November, 1943	Mormon apostle Richard R. Lyman is excommunicated for secretly practicing polygamy.
1958	Mormon apostle Bruce R. McConkie anticipates polygamy to resume. Obviously the holy practice [plural marriage] will commence again after the Second Coming of the Son of Man and the ushering in of the millennium. — Bruce R. McConkie, Mormon apostle, *Mormon Doctrine, p.578*

Doctrinal Teachings on Polygamy

When polygamy was openly practiced, Mormon authorities taught that:

- Those who reject it would be damned

   The Lord has said, that those who reject this principle reject their salvation, they shall be damned, saith the Lord; those to whom I reveal this law and they do not receive it, shall be damned. [p.224]

   I want to prophesy that all men and women who oppose the revelation which God has given in relation to polygamy will find themselves in darkness; the Spirit of God will withdraw from them from the very moment of their opposition to that principle, until they will finally go down to hell and be damned, if they do not repent. [p.225]
   — Orson Pratt, Mormon apostle, *Journal of Discourses 17:224-225*

1 Verily, thus saith the Lord... as touching the principle and doctrine of... having many wives and concubines—

2 Behold, and lo, I am the Lord thy God, and will answer thee as touching this matter.

3 Therefore, prepare thy heart to receive and obey the instructions which I am about to give unto you; for all those who have this law revealed unto them must obey the same.

4 For behold, I reveal unto you a new and an everlasting covenant; and if ye abide not that covenant, then are ye damned; for no one can reject this covenant and be permitted to enter into my glory.

5 For all who will have a blessing at my hands shall abide the law which was appointed for that blessing, and the conditions thereof, as were instituted from before the foundation of the world.

6 And as pertaining to the new and everlasting covenant, it was instituted for the fulness of my glory; and he that receiveth a fulness thereof must and shall abide the law, or he shall be damned, saith the Lord God.

— *Doctrine and Covenants, Section 132*

- It is a requirement to obtain the highest exaltation—becoming gods

The only men who become Gods, even the Sons of God, are those who enter into polygamy.

— Brigham Young, Mormon prophet, *Journal of Discourses 11:269*

Some people have supposed that the doctrine of plural marriage was a sort of superfluity, or nonessential to the salvation or exaltation of mankind. In other words, some of the Saints have said, and believe, that a man with one wife, sealed to him by the authority of the Priesthood for time and eternity, will receive an exaltation as great and glorious, if he is faithful, as he possibly could with more than one. I want here to enter my solemn protest against this idea, for I know it is false ... [p.28]

... it is useless to tell me that there is no blessing attached to obedience to the law, or that a man with only one wife can obtain as great a reward, glory or kingdom as he can with more than one, being equally faithful.[p.29-30]
— Joseph F. Smith, Mormon prophet, *Journal of Discourses 20:28-30*

- If polygamy is not true then neither is celestial marriage

If plurality of marriage is not true or in other words, if a man has no divine right to marry two wives or more in this world, then marriage for eternity is not true, and your faith is all vain, and all the sealing ordinances and powers, pertaining to marriages for eternity are vain, worthless, good for nothing; for as sure as one is true the other also must be true. Amen.
— Orson Pratt, Mormon apostle, *Journal of Discourses 21:296*

- That polygamy will exist in the afterlife

I bear my solemn testimony that plural marriage is as true as any principle that has been revealed from the heavens. I bear my testimony that it is a necessity, and that the Church of Christ in its fullness never existed without it. Where you have the eternity of marriage you are bound to have plural marriage; bound to; and it is one of the marks of the Church of Jesus Christ in its sealing ordinances.
— George Teasdale, Mormon apostle, *Journal of Discourses 25:21*

- That God the Father is a polygamist

The Scripture says that He, the Lord, came walking in the Temple, with His train; I do no know who they were, unless His wives and children...
— Brigham Young, Mormon prophet, *Journal of Discourses 13:309*

Priesthood

The Mormon church teaches that only its worthy male members possess the Aaronic and Melchizedek priesthood today, and with it comes God's exclusive authority to administer the ordinances of the gospel (i.e. baptism, healing, sacrament, preaching, etc.) Since the Aaronic and Melchizedek priesthoods are Biblical concepts, it is imperative to understand their Biblical origins.

Aaronic/Levitical Priesthood

In Judaism (aka *Old Covenant*, *Old Testament*, the *Law*) Aaron and his sons were set apart from the twelve tribes to perform service in the tabernacle, and later the temple.

- The priestly duty was restricted to the lineage of Aaron and passed down to his descendants. Exodus 30:21, Numbers 3:32,18:6-7
- Aaron was the initial high priest (Exodus 30:10), a position of oversight and responsibility including entering the 'Holy of Holies' once a year (Leviticus 16:34, Hebrews 9:7). This position also passed down to the lineal successor. Exodus 29:29, Numbers 20:26,28

In Christianity (aka *New Covenant*, *New Testament*, the *Gospel*) the death and resurrection of Jesus Christ fulfilled the Judaic system, which made obsolete its priestly offices.

- Christ's death is the last and final sacrifice. Hebrews 7:27, 10:10
- The New Covenant rendered the Old Covenant obsolete. Hebrews 7:22,8:6,13,9:15,10:9
- Furthermore, to ensure the end of the Judaic model, Christ prophesied that Jerusalem and the Jewish temple would be destroyed (fulfilled in 70 A.D.). Luke 19:41-44, 21:5-6, Matthew 24:1-2, Mark 13:1-2

- In the New Covenant, all believers in Christ (men, women, Jew, Gentile) are priests. 1 Peter 2:9, Revelation 1:6
- In the New Covenant, all believers in Christ offer spiritual sacrifices. Romans 12:1, Hebrews 13:15, 1 Peter 2:5
- Jesus Christ is the only High Priest today. Hebrews 2:17,3:1,4:14,7:26,8:1,9:11

Jesus has become the guarantee of a better covenant. The former priests, on the one hand, existed in greater numbers because they were prevented by death from continuing, but Jesus, on the other hand, because He continues forever, holds His priesthood permanently. Therefore He is able also to save forever those who draw near to God through Him, since He always lives to make intercession for them. For it was fitting for us to have such a high priest, holy, innocent, undefiled, separated from sinners and exalted above the heavens; who does not need daily, like those high priests, to offer up sacrifices, first for His own sins and then for the sins of the people, because this He did once for all when He offered up Himself. For the Law appoints men as high priests who are weak, but the word of the oath, which came after the Law, appoints a Son, made perfect forever. Now the main point in what has been said is this: we have such a high priest, who has taken His seat at the right hand of the throne of the Majesty in the heavens... But now He has obtained a more excellent ministry, by as much as He is also the mediator of a better covenant, which has been enacted on better promises. For if that first covenant had been faultless, there would have been no occasion sought for a second... When He said, "A new covenant," He has made the first obsolete but whatever is becoming obsolete and growing old is ready to disappear.
— *Hebrews 7:22-8:1,6-7,13*

Conclusion

Christ rendered the Aaronic/Levitical priesthood obsolete, and the destruction of the Jewish temple in 70 A.D. guaranteed it.

- There is no Biblical evidence in the Christian era (post-Resurrection) and in the writings of the early church fathers that Christians were ordained into the Aaronic/Levitical priesthood.
- That the sitting High Priest persecuted Christians is evidence that the Judaic priestly offices were not carried over into Christianity. Persecution of:
    - The Apostles (Acts 5:17-18)
    - Paul (Acts 23-24)
    - Jesus Christ (Matthew 26:57-68)
- The Book of Mormon does not mention the Aaronic/Levitical priesthood. This is consistent with its own narrative, as Lehi (the Nephite/Lamanite patriarch) was of the tribe of Manasseh (Alma 10:3), thus his lineage was restricted from the Aaronic/Levitical priesthood.
- There is no basis in the Bible or Book of Mormon that justifies a modern Aaronic priesthood.

Melchizedek

In Judaism, the Book of Genesis mentions a priest/king named Melchizedek. There is no other Biblical evidence of anyone practicing or being ordained into a "Melchizedek priesthood". Only four verses mention him:

- Three—his introduction in the book of Genesis. Genesis 14:18-20
- One—a messianic prophecy linking Jesus Christ to the "order of Melchizedek". Psalm 110:4

In Christianity, Chapter 7 of the book of Hebrews explains the "order of Melchizedek": how he was superior in position over the Aaronic priests; and how Jesus Christ uniquely fulfills this prophetic type and shadow of a priest/king.

- Jesus Christ was not ordained into the Aaronic priesthood since He was of the tribe of Judah. Heb. 7:14
- Since Christ fulfilled the position of the Aaronic high priest, it was necessary for another priesthood superior than the Aaronic: hence the "order of Melchizedek"—which itself was modeled after Christ. Heb. 7:3
- Melchizedek is superior:
    - He predates Aaron. Heb. 7:1
    - Through Abraham the Levites paid tithes to Melchizedek. Heb. 7:4-10
    - "Melchizedek" translated means "King of Righteousness", a title suitable to Christ. Heb. 7:2
    - Melchizedek was unique in that he was a priest and a king: "King of Salem" (which is Jeru-*salem*), when translated means "King of Peace", both titles suitable to Christ. Heb. 7:2
    - Unlike the Aaronic which required lineal succession, Melchizedek had no genealogical record and thus no lineal restriction. Heb. 7:3
    - Unlike the Aaronic where one's priestly service ended upon death (Heb. 7:23), Melchizedek had no record of birth or death, thus is likened to Jesus who has "no beginning of days nor end of life" and thus is able to serve as priest perpetually. Heb. 7:3
- The fulfillment of the Old Covenant requires a new priesthood. Heb. 7:12
- Christ, who is perfect, is the ultimate priest Heb. 7:28

Conclusion

There is no Biblical evidence in Judaism or Christianity that persons were ordained into a "Melchizedek priesthood"—other than Jesus Christ, who is the only person uniquely qualified to fulfill the prophetic type of the priest/king Melchizedek.

The Mormon Priesthoods

David Whitmer, one of the Book of Mormon witnesses, discredited the Mormon priesthoods:

- They were man made positions, originating with Sidney Rigdon.

  > This matter of the two orders of priesthood in the Church of Christ, and lineal priesthood of the old law being in the church, all originated in the mind of Sidney Rigdon. (p.64)

  > The next grievous error which crept into the church was in ordaining high priests in June, 1831. This error was introduced at the instigation of Sydney Rigdon. The office of high priest was never spoken of, and never thought of being established in the church until Rigdon came in. (p.35)
  > — David Whitmer, Mormon apostle and Book of Mormon witness, *An Address To All Believers In Christ*

- They were not practiced by the early Mormon church. According to D&C 107:7, Elders are a position under the Melchizedek Priesthood, however the church historical records show it had ordained Elders prior to the introduction of the Melchizedek Priesthood.

  > The authority of the Melchizedek Priesthood was manifested and conferred for the first time upon several of the Elders.
  > — *History of the Church, 1:175-176*

- Original revelations were edited to insert additional language to make it appear as though the church had these positions from the beginning.

> ...in a few years those revelations were changed to admit this high office, which otherwise would have condemned it. They were changed to mean something entirely different from the way they were first given and printed in the Book of Commandments; as if God had not thought of this great and important office when he gave those revelations...
> — David Whitmer, Mormon apostle and Book of Mormon witness, *An Address To All Believers In Christ*, p.46

The Edited Revelations

An examination of the earliest revelations confirm David Whitmer's criticism that the revelations were edited to make it seem like the priesthood was part of the Mormon church from the beginning.

Timeline

1829	1833	1842
Joseph Smith was allegedly ordained to the Aaronic priesthood	Revelations published with no mention of priesthoods or Joseph's ordination	First ever mention of Joseph ordination 13 years after-the-fact

- **Doctrine and Covenants, Section 2**

    Section 2 is absent in the first two editions (1833, 1835), and was inserted afterwards and back dated to make it seem that the angel Moroni had promised the priesthood in 1823.

- **Doctrine and Covenants, Section 13**

    This "revelation" that Joseph Smith received the Aaronic Priesthood is not in any of the earliest editions of the Doctrine and Covenants. In fact it wasn't published until 13 years after the event and back dated to May 15, 1829.

- **Doctrine and Covenants, Section 20**

    Three verses were added to the original revelation on church organization concerning the priesthood.

- **Doctrine and Covenants, Section 27**

    The original revelation was edited to insert language that Joseph Smith had already received the priesthood years earlier.

There is no record that Joseph Smith ever received the Melchizedek Priesthood.

> The promise to confer upon Joseph and Oliver the Melchisedek Priesthood was fulfilled; but as there is no definite account of the event in the history of the Prophet Joseph, or, for matter of that, in any of our annals.
> — B. H. Roberts, Mormon Seventy and LDS church historian, *History of the Church 1:40*

Conclusion

While the names are biblical, the modern Mormon priesthoods are not.

Racism

The Mormon church has a long history of institutionalized racism.

- Its scriptures teach that dark skin is a curse and white skin is delightsome
- The church denied blacks the priesthood
- Church authorities opposed abolishing slavery
- Church authorities opposed the Civil Rights Movement
- Church authorities opposed interracial marriages

Racism in Mormon scriptures

Mormon scripture places an emphasis on skin color. White skin is considered delightsome and dark skin a curse from God.

> And he had caused the cursing to come upon them, yea, even a sore cursing, because of their iniquity. For behold, they had hardened their hearts against him, that they had become like unto a flint; wherefore, as they were white, and exceedingly fair and delightsome, that they might not be enticing unto my people the Lord God did cause a skin of blackness to come upon them.
> — 2 Nephi 5:21

> And then shall they rejoice; for they shall know that it is a blessing unto them from the hand of God; and their scales of darkness shall begin to fall from their eyes; and many generations shall not pass away among them, save they shall be a *white and a delightsome people.
> — 2 Nephi 30:6
> * "white" was changed to "pure" in 1981

O my brethren, I fear that unless ye shall repent of your sins that their skins will be whiter than yours, when ye shall be brought with them before the throne of God. Wherefore, a commandment I give unto you, which is the word of God, that ye revile no more against them because of the darkness of their skins; neither shall ye revile against them because of their filthiness; but ye shall remember your own filthiness, and remember that their filthiness came because of their fathers.
— *Jacob 3:8-9*

And the skins of the Lamanites were dark, according to the mark which was set upon their fathers, which was a curse upon them because of their transgression and their rebellion against their brethren, who consisted of Nephi, Jacob, and Joseph, and Sam, who were just and holy men.
— *Alma 3:6*

And their curse was taken from them, and their skin became white like unto the Nephites.
— *3 Nephi 2:15*

And also that the seed of this people may more fully believe his gospel, which shall go forth unto them from the Gentiles; for this people shall be scattered, and shall become a dark, a filthy, and a loathsome people, beyond the description of that which ever hath been amongst us, yea, even that which hath been among the Lamanites, and this because of their unbelief and idolatry.
— *Mormon 5:15*

For behold, the Lord shall curse the land with much heat, and the barrenness thereof shall go forth forever; and there was a blackness came upon all the children of Canaan, that they were despised among all people.
— *Moses 7:8*

And Enoch also beheld the residue of the people which were the sons of Adam; and they were a mixture of all the seed of Adam save it was the seed of Cain, for the seed of Cain were black, and had not place among them.
— *Moses 7:22*

Blacks denied the Mormon priesthood

Mormons are taught that Cain's mark in Genesis 4:15 is the result of God cursing him with dark skin, making Cain the first black man.

- Since Cain lived before Noah's flood, a Mormon authority explains how blacks survived it.

  As a result of his rebellion, Cain was cursed with a dark skin; he became the father of the Negroes, and those spirits who are not worthy to receive the priesthood are born through this lineage...

  Noah's son Ham married *Egypt, a descendant of Cain, thus preserving the Negro lineage through the flood.
  — Bruce R. McConkie, Mormon apostle, *Mormon Doctrine, p.102,477*
  *Note: The Bible and Book of Mormon do not mention Egypt.

- This explanation is derived from the Book of Abraham, which also denies the priesthood to the descendents of Ham.

  Now this king of Egypt was a descendant from the loins of Ham, and was a partaker of the blood of the Canaanites by birth. From this descent sprang all the Egyptians, and thus the blood of the Canaanites was preserved in the land. The land of Egypt being first discovered by a woman, who was the daughter of Ham, and the daughter of Egyptus, which in the Chaldean signifies Egypt, which signifies that which is forbidden; When this woman discovered the land it was under water, who afterward settled her sons in it; and

thus, from Ham, sprang that race which preserved the curse in the land... Now, Pharaoh being of that lineage by which he could not have the right of Priesthood, notwithstanding the Pharaohs would fain claim it from Noah, through Ham, therefore my father was led away by their idolatry.
— *Abraham 1:21-24,27*

- Additional statements from general authorities.

In the evening debated with John C. Bennett and others to show that the Indians have greater cause to complain of the treatment of the whites, than the Negroes, or sons of Cain.
— Joseph Smith, Mormonism founder, *History of the Church 4:501*

You see some classes of the human family that are black, uncouth, un-comely, disagreeable and low in their habits, wild, and seemingly deprived of nearly all the blessings of the intelligence that is generally bestowed upon mankind. The first man that committed the odious crime of killing one of his brethren will be cursed the longest of any one of the children of Adam. Cain slew his brother. Cain might have been killed, and that would have put a termination to that line of human beings. This was not to be, and the Lord put a mark upon him, which is the flat nose and black skin.
— Brigham Young, Mormon prophet, *Journal of Discourses 7:290*

What was that mark? It was a mark of blackness. That mark rested upon Cain, and descended upon his posterity from that time until the present. Today there are millions of descendants of Cain, through the lineage of Ham, in the world, and that mark of darkness still rests upon them.
— Wilford Woodruff, Mormon prophet, *Discourse delivered at the General Conference, April 7, 1889, Millennial Star 51:339*

...the offspring of Ham inherited a curse, and it was because, as a revelation teaches, some of the blood of Cain became mingled with that of Ham's family, and hence they inherited that curse.
— Erastus Snow, Mormon apostle, *Journal of Discourses 21:370*

The negro is an unfortunate man. He has been given a black skin... But that is as nothing compared with that greater handicap that he is not permitted to receive the Priesthood and the ordinances of the temple, necessary to prepare men and women to enter into and enjoy a fulness of glory in the celestial kingdom.
— George F. Richards, Mormon apostle, *Conference Report, April 1939*

From the days of the Prophet Joseph even until now, it has been the doctrine of the Church, never questioned by any of the Church leaders, that the Negros are not entitled to the full blessings of the Gospel.
— George Albert Smith, Mormon prophet, *First Presidency letter dated June 16, 1947 to Dr. Lowry Nelson*

Not only was Cain called upon to suffer, but because of his wickedness he became the father of an inferior race... (p.101)

Ham, through Egypt, continued the curse which was placed upon the seed of Cain. Because of that curse this dark race was separated and isolated from all the rest of Adam's posterity before the flood, and since that time the same condition has continued, and they have been 'despised among all people.' This doctrine did not originate with President Brigham Young but was taught by the Prophet Joseph Smith... we all know it is due to his teachings that the negro today is barred from the Priesthood. (p.110-111)
— Joseph Fielding Smith, Mormon prophet, *The Way to Perfection*

- For over 120 years the Mormon church denied blacks its priesthood.
- On June 8, 1978, Spencer W. Kimball, the twelfth Mormon prophet, publicly announced that he had received a "revelation" to lift the ban on blacks. While the announcement, *Official Declaration 2*, is now part of the LDS canon, the revelation itself has never been published.

Opposition to abolishing slavery

Statements from general authorities and official church publications opposed to ending slavery

> Q: Are the Mormons abolitionists?
> No, unless delivering the people from priestcraft, and the priests from the power of Satan, should be considered abolition. But we do not believe in setting the Negroes free.
> — Joseph Smith, Mormonism founder, *History of the Church 3:29*

> ...and rebellious niggers in the slave states.
> — Joseph Smith, Mormonism founder, *Millennial Star 22:602*

> Trace mankind down to after the flood, and then another curse is pronounced upon the same race—that they should be the "servant of servants;" and they will be, until that curse is removed; and the Abolitionists cannot help it, nor in the least alter that decree.
> — Brigham Young, Mormon prophet, *Journal of Discourses 7:290*

> Having learned with extreme regret, that an article entitled, "Free People of Color," in the last number of the Star has been misunderstood, we feel in duty bound to state, in this Extra, that our intention was not only to stop free people of color from emigrating to this state, but to prevent them from being admitted as member of the Church.
> — Joseph Smith, Mormonism founder, *History of the Church, 1:378-379*

The descendents of Ham, besides a black skin which has ever been a curse that has followed an apostate of the holy priesthood, as well as a black heart, have been servants to both Shem and Japheth, and the abolitionists are trying to make void the curse of God, but it will require more power than man possesses to counteract the decrees of eternal wisdom.
— *Official LDS periodical, Times and Seasons 6:857*

Horace Greeley

Horace Greeley was an abolitionist, a Republican, and the editor of the New York Tribune. During a visit to Salt Lake City in 1859, he interviewed Brigham Young, the president of the LDS church. The following is an excerpt from the interview and comments related to Greeley's visit.

Greeley: What is the position of your church with respect to slavery?

Young: We consider it a divine institution, and not be abolished until the curse pronounced on Ham shall have been removed from his descendents.

Greeley: Are any slaves now held in this [Utah] territory?

Young: There are.

Greeley: Do your territorial laws uphold slavery?

Young: Those laws are printed—you can read for yourself. If slaves are brought here by those who owned them in the states, we do not favor their escape from the service of those owners.
— Brigham Young, Mormon prophet, *Interview with Horace Greeley, Salt Lake City, Utah, July 13, 1859*

- Comments from General Authorities on Horace Greeley's visit.

> Mr. Greeley was disappointed in the lack of abolition sentiment in Salt Lake City.
> — B. H. Roberts, Mormon apostle and LDS church historian, *Comprehensive History of the Church 4:533*

> This Greeley is one of their popular characters in the East, and one that supports the stealing of Niggers...
> — John Taylor, Mormon prophet, *Journal of Discourses 5:119*

> The rank, rabid abolitionists, whom I call black-hearted Republicans, have set the whole national fabric on fire.
> — Brigham Young, Mormon prophet, *Journal of Discourses 10:110*

Opposition to the Civil Rights Movement

The discussion on civil rights, especially over the last twenty years has drawn some very sharp lines. It has blinded the thinking of some of our own people, I believe. They have allowed their political affiliations to color their thinking to some extent, and then, of course, they have been persuaded, by some of the arguments that have been put forth...

When He placed the mark upon Cain, He engaged in segregation. When he told Enoch not to preach the gospel to the descendents of Cain who were black, the Lord engaged in segregation. When He cursed the descendants of Cain as to the Priesthood, He engaged in segregation...

I think the Lord segregated the Negro and who is man to change that segregation? It reminds me of the scripture on marriage, "what God hath joined together, let no man put asunder." Only here we have the reverse of the thing—what God hath separated, let no man bring together again.
— Mark E. Petersen, Mormon apostle, *Race Problems - As They Affect The Church*

What are we doing to fight it? Before I left for Europe I warned how the communists were using the civil rights movement to promote revolution and eventual takeover of this country. When are we going to wake up? What do you know about the dangerous civil rights agitation in Mississippi! do you fear the destruction of all vestiges of state government?

Now brethren, the Lord never promised there would not be traitors in the Church. We have the ignorant, the sleepy and the deceived who provide temptations and avenues of apostasy for the unwary and the unfaithful, but we have a prophet at our head and he has spoken. Now what are we going to do about it?

Do Homework

Brethren, if we had done our homework and were faithful we could step forward at this time and help save this country.
— Ezra Taft Benson, Mormon prophet, *135th Annual Conference*
Note: the italicized words were omitted from this speech when reprinted in the *Improvement Era*, June 1965, p.539

Opposition to Interracial Marriage

Shall I tell you the law of God in regard to the African race? If the white man who belongs to the chosen seed mixes his blood with the seed of Cain, the penalty, under the law of God, is death on the spot. This will always be so.
— Brigham Young, Mormon prophet, *Journal of Discourses 10:110*

And if any man mingle his seed with the seed of Cain the only way he could get rid of it or have Salvation would be to come forward and have his head cut off and spill his blood upon the ground—it would also take the life of his children
— Wilford Woodruff, Mormon prophet, *Personal diary 4:97*

From this and other interviews I have read, it appears that the Negro seeks absorption with the white race. He will not be satisfied until he achieves it by intermarriage. This is his objective and we must face it...

...the Negroes we have the definite word of the Lord himself that He placed a dark skin upon them: as a curse—as a sign to all others. He forbade inter-marriage with them under threat of extension of the curse...

Now what is our policy in regard to intermarriage? As to the Negro, of course, there is only one possible answer. We must not intermarry with the Negro...

What is our advice with respect to intermarriage with Chinese, Japanese, Hawaiians and so on? I will tell you what advice I give personally. If a boy or girl comes to me claiming to be in love with a Chinese or Japanese or a Hawaiian or a person of any other dark race, I do my best to talk them out of it... I teach against inter-marriage of all kinds.
— Mark E. Petersen, Mormon apostle, *Race Problems - As They Affect The Church*

Christianity

- God instructed the Apostle Peter to regard no man as unclean.

    And he said unto them, Ye know how that it is an unlawful thing for a man that is a Jew to keep company, or come unto one of another nation; but God hath shewed me that I should not call any man common or unclean.
    — *Acts 10:28*

    Then Peter opened his mouth, and said, Of a truth I perceive that God is no respecter of persons.
    — *Acts 10:34*

- Niger, a likely African, was a recognized prophet/teacher.

    Now there were in the church that was at Antioch certain prophets and teachers; as Barnabas, and Simeon that was called Niger, and Lucius of Cyrene, and Manaen, which had been brought up with Herod the tetrarch, and Saul.
    — *Acts 13:1*

- Philip baptized an Ethiopian.

> And the angel of the Lord spake unto Philip, saying, Arise, and go toward the south unto the way that goeth down from Jerusalem unto Gaza, which is desert. And he arose and went: and, behold, a man of Ethiopia, an eunuch of great authority under Candace queen of the Ethiopians, who had the charge of all her treasure, and had come to Jerusalem for to worship, And as they went on their way, they came unto a certain water: and the eunuch said, See, here is water; what doth hinder me to be baptized? And he commanded the chariot to stand still: and they went down both into the water, both Philip and the eunuch; and he baptized him.
>
> — *Acts 8:26-38*

Salvation

To understand the LDS view of salvation it is helpful to first understand these LDS doctrines:

- God was once a mortal man
- God possess a body of flesh and bones
- God is married to a Heavenly Mother(s)
- Mormons may become Gods

Pre-earth Life

Mormonism teaches that humans exist first as spirit babies—the offspring of God the Father and his wife(s). Spirit babies are sent down to earth and given a body through the conception of human parents.

> Man was also in the beginning with God...
> — *Doctrine and Covenants 93:29*

Further complicating this doctrine is the notion that God has populated other planets with his children.

> We are not the only people that the Lord has created. We have brothers and sisters on other earths. They look like us because they, too, are the children of God and were created in his image, for they are also his offspring.
> — Joseph Fielding Smith, Mormon prophet, *Doctrines of Salvation 1:62*

Lucifer

Mormonism teaches that Jesus Christ, the first born spirit baby, was appointed to be the Savior of mankind. Lucifer, the second born spirit baby (thus the brother of Jesus Christ) rebelled as he wanted to be the Savior. This caused a split: those who followed God and Jesus were permitted to come to earth and experience mortality; those who followed Lucifer were expelled and forever denied a physical body.

- The name *Lucifer* comes from an improper translation in the King James Version, which name only appears once, in Isaiah 14:12. Modern translations correct this, as the passage does not refer to the devil, but to the king of Babylon. That the Book of Mormon repeats the KJV error (2 Nephi 24:12) is evidence against its alleged ancient origin and inspired "translation".

In LDS doctrine, the punishment of being denied a physical body is severe, as a body is a prerequisite to receive exaltation. See Doctrine and Covenants 93:33-34

- Since a physical body is necessary to receive exaltation, it creates an inconsistency in LDS doctrine, as Jesus Christ was a god before his physical conception through Mary. Another difficulty is how the Holy Ghost is a god without a body of flesh and bones.

Atonement at Gethsemane

Citing Luke 22:44, Mormonism teaches that the atonement began in the garden of Gethsemane, contrary to Christ's apostles who teach that the atonement was on the cross.

- It is interesting to note that for such an important LDS doctrine: the Book of Mormon, Doctrine and Covenants and Pearl of Great Price are silent about Gethsemane.

Three Heavens: Three Degrees of Glory

Citing 2 Corinthians 12:2, Mormonism teaches that there are three heavens, with each level constituting a higher degree of glory.

After death, mankind waits for judgment day in one of two places:
- Paradise—a temporary abode of happiness and peace reserved for obedient Mormons.
- Spirit Prison—also called *hell*, for non-Mormons. Here spirits can accept Mormonism and transfer to Paradise, provided they were baptized by proxy.

Judgment day will determine where mankind will reside for eternity:
- Heaven—which is comprised of three levels:
  - Celestial Glory—reserved for the most obedient Mormons who fulfilled certain duties like priesthood, temple marriages, etc. This level has full access to Heavenly Father and Jesus Christ. Mormons who obtain this level become a God and start the cycle again by conceiving spirit babies to populate their own planets.
  - Terrestrial Glory—reserved for good people (including Mormons) who didn't quit live up to expectations. There is only access to Jesus Christ and not Heavenly Father.
  - Telestial Glory—reserved for those in spirit prison.
- Perdition—reserved for those who reject Jesus Christ, including Lucifer and his followers.

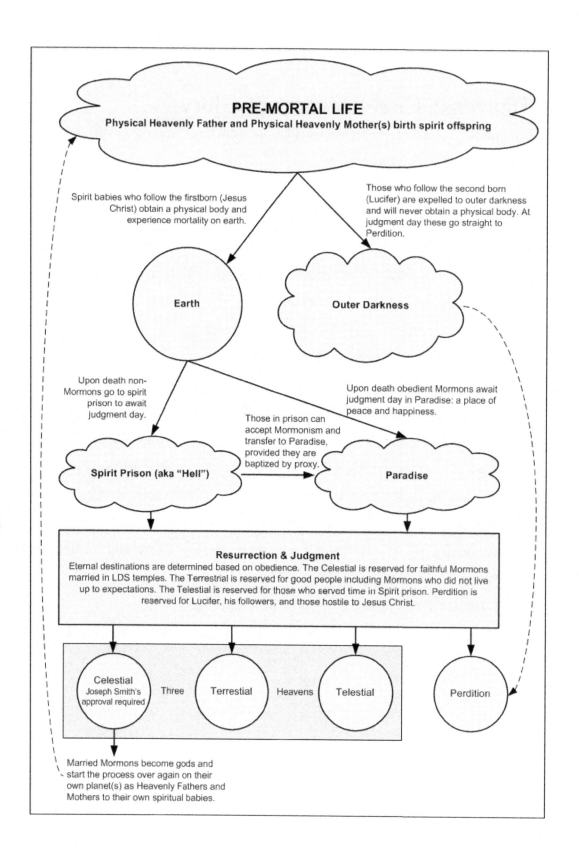

Saved by Works

Mormonism teaches that in order to obtain the highest degree of glory (Celestial), one must perform various works (i.e. obtain the priesthood, temple endowments and temple weddings, etc.) and be obedient to rules (i.e. tithing, word of wisdom, etc.).

> We believe that through the Atonement of Christ, all mankind may be saved, by obedience to the laws and ordinances of the Gospel.
> — Joseph Smith, Mormon founder, *Article of Faith #3*

> For we labor diligently to write, to persuade our children, and also our brethren, to believe in Christ, and to be reconciled to God; for we know that it is by grace that we are saved, <u>after all we can do</u>.*
> — *2 Nephi 25:23*
> * *How do we know if we have done 'all we can do'?*

Salvation through Joseph Smith

Mormonism teaches that salvation comes through Joseph Smith.

> No man or woman in this dispensation will ever enter into the celestial kingdom of God without the consent of Joseph Smith... every man and woman must have the certificate of Joseph Smith, junior, as a passport to their entrance into the mansion where God and Christ are.
> — Brigham Young, Mormon prophet, *Journal of Discourses 7:289*

> I tell you, Joseph holds the keys, and none of us can get into the celestial kingdom without passing by him... If brother Joseph is satisfied with you, you may pass. If it is all right with him, it is all right with me.
> — Orson Hyde, Mormon apostle, *Journal of Discourses 6:154-155*

Every spirit that confesses that Joseph Smith is a Prophet, that he lived and died a Prophet and that the Book of Mormon is true, is of God, and every spirit that does not is of anti-Christ.
— Brigham Young, Mormon prophet, *History of the Church 7:287*

Every intelligent person under the heavens that does not, when informed, acknowledge that Joseph Smith, Jun., is a Prophet of God, is in darkness, and is opposed to us and to Jesus and his kingdom on the earth.
— Brigham Young, Mormon prophet, *Journal of Discourses 8:223*

Believe in God, believe in Jesus, and believe in Joseph his Prophet, and in Brigham his successor. And I add, "If you will believe in your heart and confess with your mouth that Jesus is the Christ, that Joseph was a Prophet, and that Brigham was his successor, you shall be saved in the kingdom of God," which I pray, in the name of Jesus, may be the case. Amen.
— Joseph Young, Mormon Seventy, *Journal of Discourses 6:229*

Joseph Smith, the Prophet and Seer of the Lord, has done more, save Jesus only, for the salvation of men in this world, than any other man that ever lived in it.
— *Doctrine and Covenants 135:3*

Christianity—Salvation in Christ alone

And there is salvation in no one else; for there is no other name under heaven that has been given among men by which we must be saved.
— *Acts 4:12*

Jesus said to him, "I am the way, and the truth, and the life; no one comes to the Father but through Me."
— *John 14:6*

Salvation by faith not works

Jesus Christ's apostles teach that salvation is a gift obtained through faith alone in Jesus Christ, and that good works are a natural response to this gift.

> For by grace you have been saved through faith; and that not of yourselves, it is the gift of God; not as a result of works, so that no one may boast. For we are His workmanship, created in Christ Jesus for good works, which God prepared beforehand so that we would walk in them.
> — *Ephesians 2:8-10*

> For we maintain that a man is justified by faith apart from the works of the law.
> — *Romans 3:28*

> He has saved us and called us with a holy calling, not according to our works, but according to His own purpose and grace which was granted us in Christ Jesus from all eternity.
> — *2 Timothy 1:9*

> Therefore they said to Him, "What shall we do, so that we may work the works of God?" Jesus answered and said to them, "This is the work of God, that you believe in Him whom He has sent."
> — *John 6:28-29*

> For it is with your heart that you believe and are justified, and it is with your mouth that you profess your faith and are saved.
> — *Romans 10:10*

The apostle Paul teaches that some Jews did not receive salvation because they tried to earn it through their works. A person who attempts to obtain salvation from their own good works becomes a Christ to themselves.

> What then shall we say? That the Gentiles, who did not pursue righteousness, have obtained it, a righteousness that is by faith; but the people of Israel, who pursued the law as the way of righteousness, have not attained their goal. Why not? Because they pursued it not by faith but as if it were by works. They stumbled over the stumbling stone... Brothers and sisters, my heart's desire and prayer to God for the Israelites is that they may be saved. For I can testify about them that they are zealous for God, but their zeal is not based on knowledge. Since they did not know the righteousness of God and sought to establish their own, they did not submit to God's righteousness. Christ is the culmination of the law so that there may be righteousness for everyone who believes.
> — *Romans 9:31-32, 10:1-4*

Atonement on the Cross

The apostles of Christ's time taught that the atonement took place on the cross. There is no teaching that the atonement started in the garden of Gethsemane.

> And through him to reconcile to himself all things, whether things on earth or things in heaven, by making peace through his blood, shed on the cross.
> — *Colossians 1:20*

And He Himself bore our sins in His body on the cross, so that we might die to sin and live to righteousness...
— *1 Peter 2:24*

Having canceled out the certificate of debt consisting of decrees against us, which was hostile to us; and He has taken it out of the way, having nailed it to the cross.
— *Colossians 2:14*

For the word of the cross is foolishness to those who are perishing, but to us who are being saved it is the power of God.
— *1 Corinthians 1:18*

- Note: the Book of Mormon, Doctrine and Covenants and Pearl of Great Price do not mention *Gethsemane*.

Man Created—not Conceived

He was saying to them, "You are from below, I am from above; you are of this world, I am not of this world."
— *John 8:23*

"He who comes from above is above all, he who is of the earth is from the earth and speaks of the earth. He who comes from heaven is above all."
— *John 3:31*

...Thus declares the LORD who stretches out the heavens, lays the foundation of the earth, and forms the spirit of man within him.
— *Zechariah 12:1*

> Then the LORD God formed man of dust from the ground, and breathed into his nostrils the breath of life; and man became a living being.
> — *Genesis 2:7*

> There was Rebekah also, when she had conceived twins by one man, our father Isaac; for though the twins were not yet born and had not done anything good or bad...
> — *Romans 9:10-12*

- Furthermore, the Bible, Book of Mormon, Doctrine and Covenants and Pearl of Great Price do not mention Heavenly mother(s).

Jesus created Satan (Lucifer)

The apostles of biblical times teach that Jesus is creator of all. That Lucifer is the spirit brother of Jesus is heretical.

> For by Him all things were created, both in the heavens and on earth, visible and invisible, whether thrones or dominions or rulers or authorities — all things have been created through Him and for Him.
> — *Colossians 1:16*

> All things came into being through Him, and apart from Him nothing came into being that has come into being.
> — *John 1:3*

> For from Him and through Him and to Him are all things to Him be the glory forever. Amen.
> — *Romans 11:36*

Yet for us there is but one God, the Father, from whom are all things and we exist for Him; and one Lord, Jesus Christ, by whom are all things, and we exist through Him.
— *1 Corinthians 8:6*

The Biblical Three Heavens

The apostles and prophets of biblical times do teach that there are three heavens. However their definitions are not the same as modern Mormonism.

The First Heaven: Earth's atmosphere

God made the expanse, and separated the waters which were below the expanse from the waters which were above the expanse; and it was so. God called the expanse heaven. And there was evening and there was morning, a second day.
— *Genesis 1:7-8*

I looked, and behold, there was no man, and all the birds of the heavens had fled.
— *Jeremiah 4:25*

...He will shut up the heavens so that there will be no rain and the ground will not yield its fruit...
— *Deuteronomy 11:17*

...He did good and gave you rains from heaven and fruitful seasons...
— *Acts 14:17*

The Second Heaven: the Universe

> ...I will greatly multiply your seed as the stars of the heavens and as the sand which is on the seashore...
> — *Genesis 22:17*

> They will be exposed to the sun and the moon and all the stars of the heavens...
> — *Jeremiah 8:2*

> For the stars of heaven and their constellations Will not flash forth their light; The sun will be dark when it rises and the moon will not shed its light.
> — *Isaiah 13:10*

The Third Heaven: God's Throne and Kingdom

The scriptures teach that God transcends Heaven.

> ...Behold, heaven and the highest heaven cannot contain You...
> — *1 Kings 8:27*

> He who descended is Himself also He who ascended far above all the heavens, so that He might fill all things.
> — *Ephesians 4:10*

- Heaven is used symbolically as the place of God's throne.

> The LORD is in His holy temple; the LORD'S throne is in heaven.
> — *Psalm 11:4*

Immediately I was in the Spirit; and behold, a throne was standing in heaven, and One sitting on the throne.
— *Revelation 4:2*

New Heaven and New Earth

Jesus Christ and his apostles teach that a new Earth will be the residence of God and His believers.

"For truly I say to you, until heaven and earth pass away, not the smallest letter or stroke shall pass from the Law until all is accomplished.
— *Matthew 5:18*

"Heaven and earth will pass away, but My words will not pass away."
— *Matthew 24:35*

But the day of the Lord will come like a thief, in which the heavens will pass away with a roar and the elements will be destroyed with intense heat, and the earth and its works will be burned up. Since all these things are to be destroyed in this way, what sort of people ought you to be in holy conduct and godliness, looking for and hastening the coming of the day of God, because of which the heavens will be destroyed by burning, and the elements will melt with intense heat! But according to His promise we are looking for new heavens and a new earth, in which righteousness dwells.
— *2 Peter 3:10-13*

Then I saw a new heaven and a new earth; for the first heaven and the first earth passed away, and there is no longer any sea. And I saw the holy city, new Jerusalem, coming down out of heaven from God, made ready as a bride adorned for her husband. And I heard a loud voice from the throne, saying, "Behold, the tabernacle of God is among men, and He will dwell among them, and they shall be His people, and God Himself will be among them."

— *Revelation 21:1-3*

Temples

The Mormon church has over 130 temples around the world that are used to perform various ceremonies.

Solomon's Temple

The origin of Solomon's temple began in 1440 B.C. with the Tabernacle.

Timeline

1440 BC	957 BC	586 BC	538 BC	20 BC	70 AD
God gives Moses designs for the Tabernacle	Solomon builds the first temple	Babylonians destroy the temple	The temple is rebuilt	Herod the Great renovates the temple	Romans destroy the temple

The Tabernacle

The Tabernacle was a mobile tent and courtyard.

- Its design was given to Moses from God (Exodus 25:8-9).
- The courtyard had an altar for temporary sacrifices to atone for sins. The tent was partitioned into two rooms, separated by a thick curtain (veil).
- The back room was called the Holy of Holies which housed the Ark of the Covenant (Exodus 26:33-34).
- King Solomon built a permanent temple to replace the mobile tabernacle.
- Christ's death on the cross was the last and final sacrifice, ending the use of the temple and its regular sacrifices.

> Jesus offered one sacrifice for sins for all time...
> — *Hebrews 10:12*

- The torn veil (Mark 15:38, Matt. 27:51, Luke 23:45) exposing the Holy of Holies symbolizes that God does not dwell in man made temples but in believers. Christ's apostles teach that believers are God's temple.

> If anyone defiles the temple of God, God will destroy him. For the temple of God is holy, which temple you are.
> — *1 Corinthians 3:17*

> For we are God's fellow workers; you are God's field, God's building.
> — *1 Corinthians 3:9*

> In whom you also are being built together into a dwelling of God in the Spirit.
> — *Ephesians 2:22*

> However, you are not in the flesh but in the Spirit, if indeed the Spirit of God dwells in you, but if anyone does not have the Spirit of Christ, he does not belong to Him.
> — *Romans 8:9*

> Do you not know that your body is a temple of the Holy Spirit who is in you, whom you have from God, and that you are not your own?
> — *1 Corinthians 6:19*

The Book of Mormon echoes this teaching, but Joseph Smith contradicts it.

And this I know, because the Lord hath said he dwelleth not in unholy temples, but in the hearts of the righteous doth he dwell... — *Alma 34:36*	... the idea that the Father and the Son dwell in a man's heart is an old sectarian notion, and is false. — *Doctrine & Covenants 130:3*

- The destruction of the Jewish temple by the Romans in 70 A.D. confirmed Jesus Christ's prophecy, ending the era of the temple.

Mormon Temples

LDS Endowments

Endowments are ceremonies for a Mormon to make solemn promises of personal obedience and secrecy. An endowment is a prerequisite to both missionary service and temple marriage.

The apostles and prophets of biblical times gave no instruction for temple endowments. Likewise, the Book of Mormon is silent on this matter.

Baptisms for the dead

In subsequent endowments Mormons perform baptisms for deceased people.

In order to facilitate baptisms for the dead, the LDS church spends millions of dollars to maintain genealogy records at the massive Granite Mountain Vault (which warehouses over two billion records); and maintains over 4,500 facilities world-wide to assist those searching records.

The apostles and prophets of biblical times gave no instruction to perform baptisms for the dead. Contrary to LDS practice, they instruct that man cannot aid another's redemption and to avoid genealogies.

> Nor pay attention to myths and endless genealogies, which give rise to mere speculation rather than furthering the administration of God which is by faith.
> — *1 Timothy 1:4*

> But avoid foolish controversies and genealogies and strife and disputes about the Law, for they are unprofitable and worthless.
> — *Titus 3:9*

> No man can by any means redeem his brother or give to God a ransom for him.
> — *Psalm 49:7*

Furthermore, the Book of Mormon teaches that there are no second chances in the after life as it is impossible to change our minds.

> And now, as I said unto you before, as ye have had so many witnesses, therefore, I beseech of you that ye do not procrastinate the day of your repentance until the end; for after this day of life, which is given us to prepare for eternity, behold, if we do not improve our time while in this life, then cometh the night of darkness wherein there can be no labor performed.
>
> Ye cannot say, when ye are brought to that awful crisis, that I will repent, that I will return to my God. Nay, ye cannot say this; for that same spirit which doth possess your bodies at the time that ye go out of this life, that same spirit will have power to possess your body in that eternal world.
>
> For behold, if ye have procrastinated the day of your repentance even until death, behold, ye have become subjected to the spirit of the devil, and he doth seal you his; therefore, the Spirit of the Lord hath withdrawn from you, and hath no place in you, and the devil hath all power over you; and this is the final state of the wicked.
> — *Alma 34:33-35*

Weddings

Temples serve as facilities for exclusive Mormon weddings and non-Mormons are not allowed to participate.

The doctrine that temple weddings are an essential work is an evolution in Mormon doctrine. Marriages were conducted outside of temples for at least its first 40 years. The church altered its scriptures on this matter. See Doctrine and Covenants 101

Conclusion

There is no historical evidence or biblical teaching that Jesus Christ and his apostles instructed the Christian church to construct and perform ceremonies in temples. The notion of modern temples are not rooted in Christian teaching.

The Mormon Testimony

Mormons claim that a personal feeling, a burning in the bosom, which is interpreted to be a manifestation of the Holy Ghost, is the only evidence needed to prove that their religion is true. However virtually all religions claim to have spiritual experiences. Compare for example:

Religion	Experience
Islamism	Sufism
Buddhism	Nirvana
Hinduism	Moksha
Mormonism	Burning in bosom

Testimonies

Personal religious experiences serve as confirmation of a religion's truthfulness. These result in personal testimonies that are repeated as affirmations. Testimonies compound the verity of one's religion.

Compare for example

A common Mormon testimony	A common Muslim testimony
"I bear you my testimony that I know the Book of Mormon is true, I know that Joseph Smith is a true Prophet of God, and I know that the Church is the only true church."	"I bear witness that there is no God but Allah, and I bear witness that Mohammed is the prophet and Messenger of Allah."

In a world of diverse religions and conflicting teachings—each with spiritual experiences, we can conclude:

- All religions may be false, but all cannot be equally true
- Spiritual experiences can not be all from the same source
- Spiritual experiences do not always guarantee true teaching

Since the spiritual can be experienced in many religions, what makes the Mormon witness the true spiritual witness?

Joseph Smith

Joseph Smith was the founder of Mormonism.

- At age 20 Joseph was tried in court and found guilty for falsely claiming that he could find hidden treasure by looking at seer stones.
- When Joseph was 26 years old he claimed that at age 14 he was visited by God the Father and Jesus Christ. He also then claimed that at age 17 he was visited by an angel named Moroni, who told him of a book buried in a nearby hill that contained the history of the ancient inhabitants of the Americas. He then claimed that at age 21 he obtained the hidden book, made of gold plates, and written in reformed Egyptian, for which he also claimed to possess a supernatural ability to translate it.
- In 1830 he published the *Book of Mormon*, his alleged translation of the alleged gold plates.
- Afterwards that same year he claimed to receive a revelation that he was to be *Prophet, Seer and Revelator* of the new Mormon church.
- Three years later Joseph secretly married his second wife, on his way to taking as many as 48 wives.
- After Jane Law rebuffed Joseph Smith's proposal to marry him, her husband, William Law, was excommunicated from the church. Mr. Law was Joseph's *Second Counselor*. In protest, Austin Cowles, the *First Counselor* left the church. Both published testimonies condemning Joseph's polygamy in the *Nauvoo Expositor*. Joseph Smith then ordered that newspaper's printing press destroyed. The governor of Illinois stepped in and had Joseph put in jail, where he was killed by an angry mob in protest.

Joseph Smith—Money Digger

On March 20, 1826, four years before publishing the Book of Mormon, Joseph Smith was tried in court and found guilty for deceiving Josiah Stowel into believing that he could locate hidden treasure through divination—by peering at a stone in a hat. Joseph employed the same process to "translate" his Book of Mormon.

People of the State of New York vs. Joseph Smith.

Warrant issued upon oath of Peter G. Bridgman, who informed that one Joseph Smith of Bainbridge was a disorderly person and an imposter.

Prisoner was brought into court March 20 (1826). Prisoner examined. Says that he came from town of Palmyra, and had been at the house of Josiah Stowel in Bainbridge most of the time since; had small part of time been employed in looking for mines, but the major part had been employed by said Stowel on his farm and going to school; that he had a certain stone, which he had occasionally looked at to determine where hidden treasures in the bowels of the earth were; that he professed to tell in this manner where gold-mines were a distance under ground, and had looked for Mr. Stowel several times, and informed him where he could find those treasures, and Mr. Stowel had been engaged in digging for them; that at Palmyra he pretended to tell, by looking at this stone, where coined money was buried in Pennsylvania, and while at Palmyra he had frequently ascertained in that way where lost property was, of various kinds; that he has occasionally been in the habit of looking through this stone to find lost property for three years, but of late had pretty much given it up on account its injuring his health, especially his eyes — made them sore; that he did not solicit business of this kind, and had always rather declined having anything to do with this business.

Josiah Stowel sworn. Says that prisoner had been at his house something like five months. Had been employed by him to work on farm part of time; that he pretended to have skill of telling where hidden treasures in the earth were, by means of looking through a certain stone; that prisoner had looked for him sometimes—once to tell him about money buried on Bend Mountain in Pennsylvania, once for gold on Monument Hill, and once for a salt-spring,—and that he positively knew that the prisoner could tell, and professed the art of seeing those valuable treasures through the medium of said stone; that he found the digging part at Bend and Monument Hill as prisoner represented it; that prisoner had looked through said stone for Deacon Attelon, for a mine—did not exactly find it, but got a piece of ore, which resembled gold, he thinks; that prisoner had told by means of this stone where a Mr. Bacon had buried money; that he and prisoner had been in search of it; that prisoner said that it was in a certain root of a stump five feet from surface of the earth, and with it would be found a tail-feather; that Stowel and prisoner there upon commenced digging, found a tail-feather, but money was gone; that he supposed that money moved down; that prisoner did offer his services; that he never deceived him; that prisoner looked through stone, and described Josiah Stowel's house and out-houses while at Palmyra, at Simpson Stowel's, correctly; that he had told about a painted tree with a man's hand painted upon it, by means of said stone; that he had been in company with prisoner digging for gold and had the most implicit faith in prisoner's skill.

Horace Stowel sworn. Says he see prisoner look into hat through stone, pretending to tell where a chest of dollars were buried in Windsor, a number of miles distant; marked out size of chest in the leaves on ground.

Arad Stowel sworn. Says that he went to see whether prisoner could convince him that he possessed the skill that he professed to have, upon which prisoner laid a book open upon a white cloth, and proposed looking through another stone which was white and transparent; hold the stone to the candle, turn his back to book and read. The deception appeared so palpable, that went off disgusted.

McMaster sworn. Says he went with Arad Stowel to be convinced of prisoner's skill, and likewise came away disgusted, finding the deception so palpable. Prisoner pretended to him that he could discern objects at a distance by holding this white stone to the sun or candle; that prisoner rather declined looking into a hat at his dark-colored stone, as he said that it hurt his eyes.

Jonathan Thompson says that prisoner was requested to look Yeomans for chest of money; did look, and pretended to know where it was, and that prisoner, Thompson, and Yeo-mans went in search of it; that Smith arrived at the spot first (was in night); that Smith looked in hat while there and when very dark, and told how the chest was situated. After digging several feet, struck upon something sounding like a board or plank. Prisoner would not look again, pretending that he was alarmed the last time that he looked, on account of the circumstances relating to the trunk being buried came all fresh to his mind; that the last time that he looked, he discovered distinctly the two Indians who buried the trunk; that a quarrel ensued between them, and that one of said Indians was killed by the other, and thrown into the hole beside of the trunk, to guard it, as he supposed. Thompson says that he believes in the prisoner's professed skill; that the board which he struck his spade upon was probably the chest, but, on account of an enchantment, the trunk kept settling away from under them while digging; that, not withstanding they continued constantly removing the dirt, yet the trunk kept about the same distance from them. Says prisoner said that it appeared to him that salt might be found at Bainbridge; and that he is certain that prisoner can divine things by means of said stone and hat; that, as evidence of fact, prisoner looked into his hat to tell him about some money witness lost sixteen years ago, and that he described the man that witness supposed had taken it, and disposition of money.

And thereupon the Court finds the defendant guilty.

Justice Albert Neeley
Court Report, March 20, 1826
Reprinted in Schaff-Herzog Encyclopedia 2:1556

- Joseph acknowledged looking for buried treasure, but avoided talking about the trial.

In the month of October, 1825, I hired with an old gentleman by the name of Josiah Stowel, who lived in Chenango County, state of New York. He had heard something of a silver mine having been opened by the Spaniards in Harmony, Susquehanna county, state of Pennsylvania; and had, previous to my hiring to him, been digging, in order, if possible, to discover the mine. After I went to live with him, he took me, with the rest of his hands, to dig for the silver mine, at which I continued to work for nearly a month, without success in our undertaking, and finally I prevailed with the old gentleman to cease digging after it. Hence arose the very prevalent story of my having been a money digger.

— Joseph Smith, Mormonism founder, *History of the Church, 1:16*

- Joseph downplayed the significance of his money digging in a written Q&A:

    I answered the questions which were frequently asked me...

    Tenth—"Was not Jo Smith a money digger?"
    Answer. Yes, but it was never a very profitable job to him, as he only got fourteen dollars a month for it.
    — Joseph Smith, Mormonism founder, *Elder's Journal, Vol. 1, No. 2, p.28-29, Reprinted in the History of the Church 3:29*

Joseph Smith—Prophet

An examination of numerous prophecies given by Joseph Smith.

False Prophecies

A selection of numerous false prophecies given by Joseph Smith.

- Joseph prophesied that his generation would build a temple in Independence, Missouri. The temple has never been built and today another church, the Church of Christ, owns the temple lot.

    Which city shall be built, beginning at the temple lot, which is appointed by the finger of the Lord, in the western boundaries of the State of Missouri, and dedicated by the hand of Joseph Smith, Jun., and others with whom the Lord was well pleased. Verily this is the word of the Lord, that the city New Jerusalem shall be built by the gathering of the saints, beginning at this place, even the place of the temple, which temple shall be reared in this generation. For verily this generation shall not all pass away until an house shall be built unto the Lord, and a cloud shall rest upon it, which cloud shall be even the glory of the Lord, which shall fill the house.
    — *Doctrine and Covenants 84:3-5*

- Joseph made four false prophecies and thus were subsequently omitted from the Doctrine and Covenants 137.

I saw the *Twelve Apostles of the Lamb, who are now upon the earth, who hold the keys of this last ministry, in foreign lands, standing together in a circle, much fatigued, with their clothes tattered and their feet swollen, with their eyes cast downward, and Jesus standing in their midst, and they did not behold him. The Savior looked upon them and wept.

Note: *seven of the twelve were excommunicated or apostatized.

I also beheld Elder M'Lellin in the south, standing upon a hill, surrounded by a vast multitude, preaching to them, and a lame man standing before him supported by his crutches; he threw them down at his word and leaped as a hart, by the mighty power of God.

Note: M'Lellin was excommunicated.

Also, I saw Elder Brigham Young standing in a strange land, in the far south and west, in a desert place, upon a rock in the midst of a bout a dozen men of color, who appeared hostile. He was preaching to them in their own tongue, and the angel of God standing above his head with a drawn sword in his hand, protecting him, but he did not see it.

Note: There is no record of this at any time in Brigham's life.

And I finally saw the Twelve in the celestial kingdom of God. I also beheld the redemption of Zion [Independence, Missouri] and many things which the tongue of man cannot describe in full.

Note: since seven of the twelve had left the LDS church, according to LDS doctrine they would not all be together in the Celestial Kingdom.

— Joseph Smith, Mormonism founder, History of the Church 2:381
* John F. Boynton, Luke S. Johnson, Lyman Johnson, William E. M'Lellin, Thomas B. Marsh, Orson Hyde, William Smith.

- Joseph prophesied that the LDS church was to form a communalist program to share property and resources to help eradicate poverty. This program was called the United Order, and was prophesied to be an everlasting order until Jesus Christ's second coming. It contrast it was short lived and ultimately abandoned.

  Verily I say unto you, my friends, I give unto you counsel, and a commandment, concerning all the properties which belong to the order which I commanded to be organized and established, to be a united order, and an everlasting order for the benefit of my church, and for the salvation of men until I come.
  — Doctrine and Covenants 104:1

- On April 17, 1838, Joseph prophesied that LDS apostle David W. Patten would serve a mission the following spring. Six months later, on October 25, Patten died in the Battle of Crooked River.

  Verily thus saith the Lord: It is wisdom in my servant David W. Patten, that he settle up all his business as soon as he possibly can, and make a disposition of his merchandise, that he may perform a mission unto me next spring, in company with others, even twelve including himself, to testify of my name and bear glad tidings unto all the world.
  — Doctrine and covenants 114:1

- David Whitmer, one of the Three Witnesses said that Joseph Smith prophesied that the Book of Mormon copyright would be sold in Toronto.

  > Joseph looked into the hat in which he placed the stone, and received a revelation that some of the brethren should go to Toronto, Canada, and that they would sell the copy-right of the Book of Mormon. Hiram Page and Oliver Cowdery went to Toronto on this mission, but they failed entirely to sell the copy-right, returning without any money.
  > — David Whitmer, Mormon apostle and Book of Mormon Witness, *An Address To All Believers In Christ, p.31*

  o Joseph allegedly received a second revelation explaining why the first revelation failed:

  > Some revelations are of God: some revelations are of man: and some revelations are of the devil.
  > — Joseph Smith, Mormonism founder, *As quoted by David Whitmer in An Address To All Believers In Christ, p.31*
  >
  > Note: *If Joseph can't determine the source of revelation, why should we trust any of his revelations?*

- Joseph prophesied that unless his wife Emma accept him taking plural wives, she would be destroyed. Emma rejected it.

> And let mine handmaid, Emma Smith, receive all those that have been given unto my servant Joseph, and who are virtuous and pure before me... And I command mine handmaid, Emma Smith, to abide and cleave unto my servant Joseph, and to none else. But if she will not abide this commandment she shall be destroyed, saith the Lord; for I am the Lord thy God, and will destroy her if she abide not in my law... And if he have ten virgins given unto him by this law, he cannot commit adultery, for they belong to him, and they are given unto him; therefore is he justified.
> — *Doctrine and Covenants 132:54-55,62*
>
> *Note: despite rejecting the prophecy Emma lived to be 75 years old. It was Joseph who died 11 months after giving this prophecy.*

True Prophecy

Joseph's prophesied that a man who boasts in his own strength would incur God's vengeance.

> For although a man may have many revelations, and have power to do many mighty works, yet if he boasts in his own strength, and sets at naught the counsels of God, and follows after the dictates of his own will and carnal desires, he must fall and incur the vengeance of a just God upon him.
> — *Doctrine and Covenants 3:4*

- On May 26, 1844, Joseph made this boast about himself:

> I will come out on the top at last. I have more to boast of than ever any man had. I am the only man that has ever been able to keep a whole church together since the days of Adam. A large majority of the whole have stood by me. Neither Paul, John, Peter, nor

Jesus ever did it. I boast that no man ever did such a work as I. The followers of Jesus ran away from Him; but the Latter-day Saints never ran away from me yet.
— Joseph Smith, Mormonism founder, *History of the Church 6:408*

- Joseph's prophecy came true as one month later, on June 27, 1844, he was dead.

Testing Prophets

The prophets and apostles of biblical times warn about false prophets. They provide us criteria by which to determine false prophets.

- Prophets must be put to the test.

    Beloved, do not believe every spirit, but test the spirits to see whether they are from God, because many false prophets have gone out into the world.
    — John 1:41

- A prophet's message must be in harmony with the Gospel.

    But though we, or an angel from heaven, preach any other gospel unto you than that which we have preached unto you, let him be accursed. As we have said before, so I say again now, if any man is preaching to you a gospel contrary to what you received, he is to be accursed!
    — *Galatians 1:8-9*

- Examine the conduct of self-proclaimed prophets, do they:
    - Secretly introduce new doctrines?
    - Turn to sensuality?
    - Become greedy?
    - Exploit followers?

But false prophets also arose among the people, just as there will also be false teachers among you, who will secretly introduce destructive heresies, even denying the Master who bought them, bringing swift destruction upon themselves. Many will follow their sensuality, and because of them the way of the truth will be maligned; and in their greed they will exploit you with false words; their judgment from long ago is not idle, and their destruction is not asleep.

— *2 Peter 2:1-3*

- False prophets make false prophecies.
  See Jeremiah 28

- Those who perform signs, wonders, and even prophesy things that come true are false prophets if they teach the wrong god(s).

    If a prophet or a dreamer of dreams arises among you and gives you a sign or a wonder, and the sign or the wonder comes true, concerning which he spoke to you, saying, 'Let us go after other gods (whom you have not known) and let us serve them,' you shall not listen to the words of that prophet or that dreamer of dreams; for the LORD your God is testing you to find out if you love the LORD your God with all your heart and with all your soul.

    — *Deuteronomy 13:1-3*

Joseph Smith—Translator

Joseph Smith claimed that the Book of Mormon is his translation of reformed Egyptian. He also gave a prophecy of himself that he was a translator.

> I give unto you my servant Joseph to be a presiding elder over all my church, to be a translator, a revelator, a seer, and prophet.
> — *Doctrine and Covenants 124:125*

There are three works for which we can examine Joseph's claim of being a translator.

- **Book of Mormon**

    We are unable to directly examine Joseph's translation, as according to him, an angel kept the gold plates after his translation was completed.
    - However, when we examine the characters Joseph said he copied off the plates we can confirm they are not Egyptian (see Charles Anthon).

- **Book of Abraham**

    Egyptologists confirm that Joseph's "translation" of Egyptian papyri, which he claimed to be the writings of Abraham, is inaccurate.

- **Kinderhook Plates**

    Joseph translated a portion of brass plates that were later revealed to be a hoax.

Kinderhook Plates

Bridge Whitten, Robert Wiley and Wilbur Fugate conspired to bait Joseph Smith to see if he would translate another set of ancient plates. This time though, the plates would not come from an angel, but were deliberately engraved with gibberish characters.

- They fabricated six plates from brass, engraved "hieroglyphics" on them, and buried them in a hill in Kinderhook, Illinois.
- They orchestrated a "discovery" of the plates that were hailed as a finding of ancient records.
- The plates were then sent to Joseph Smith who fell for their trap as he provided an initial translation of them.
- Despite the hoax, for nearly 140 years Mormon periodicals and historians insisted the plates were authentically ancient.

> Church historians continued to insist on the authenticity of the Kinderhook plates until 1980 when an examination conducted by the Chicago Historical Society possessor of one plate proved it was a nineteenth-century creation.
> — Mormon historian Richard Bushman, *Rough Stone Rolling, p.490*

Timeline

April 23, 1843	Brass plates "discovered" in Kinderhook, Illinois
April 29, 1843	Plates delivered to Nauvoo, Illinois
May 1, 1843	I insert fac-similes of the six brass plates found near Kinderhook, in Pike county, Illinois, on April 23, by Mr. Robert Wiley and others, while excavating a large mound ... I have translated a portion of them, and find they contain the history of the person with whom they were found. He was a descendant of Ham, through the loins of Pharaoh, king of Egypt, and that he received his kingdom from the Ruler of heaven and earth. — Joseph Smith, Mormonism founder, *History of the Church 5:372* May 1. [Joseph Smith] Translates a portion of certain brass plates discovered at Kinderhook, Iowa — John A. Widstoe, Mormon apostle, *Joseph Smith—Seeker after Truth, Prophet of God, p.366*
May 3, 1843	Circumstances are daily transpiring which give additional testimony to the authenticity of the Book of Mormon ... The following letter and certificate, will, perhaps have a tendency to convince the skeptical, that such things have been used, and that even the obnoxious Book of Mormon, may be true; and as the people of Columbus' day were obliged to believe that there was such a place as America; so will the people in this day be obliged to believe, however reluctantly, that there may have been such plates as those from which the Book of Mormon was translated. Mr. Smith has had those plates, what his opinion concerning them is, we have not yet ascertained. The gentleman that owns them has taken them away, or we should have given a fac simile of the plates and characters in this number. We are informed however, that he purposes returning with them for translation; if so, we may be able yet to furnish our readers with it. It will be seen by the annexed statement of the Quincy Whig, that there are more dreamers and money diggers, than Joseph Smith, in the world, and the worthy editor is obliged to acknowledge that this circumstance will go a good way to prove the authenticity of the Book of Mormon. He further states that, "if Joseph Smith can decipher the hieroglyphics on the plates, he will do more towards throwing light on the early history of this continent than any man living." We think that he has done that already, in translating and publishing the Book of Mormon, and would advise the gentleman and all interested, to read for themselves, and understand. We have no doubt however, but Mr. Smith will be able to translate them. — *Times & Seasons 4:185-186*

	The plates above alluded to were exhibited in this city last week and are now we understand in Nauvoo subject to the inspection of the Mormon Prophet. The public curiosity is greatly excited and if Smith can decipher the hieroglyphics on the plates he will do more towards throwing light on the early history of this continent than any man now living. — *Quincy Whig, vol. 6, No. 2*
May 7, 1843	Six plates having the appearance of Brass have lately been dug out of a mound by a gentleman in Pike Co. Illinois. They are small and filled with engravings in Egyptian language and contain the genealogy of one of the ancient Jaredites back to Ham the son of Noah. His bones were found in the same vase (made of Cement). Part of the bones were 15 ft. underground... A large number of Citizens have seen them and compared the characters with those on the Egyptian papyrus which is now in this city. — Parley P. Pratt, Mormon apostle, *John Van Cott correspondence, LDS Archives* In the forenoon I was visited by several gentlemen, concerning the plates that were dug out near Kinderhook. — Joseph Smith, Mormonism founder, *History of the Church 5:384*
May 10, 1843	The contents of the Plates together with a Fac-Simile of the same will be published in the "Times & Seasons " as soon as the translation is completed. — *Nauvoo Neighbor, May 10, 1843*
January 15, 1844	Why does the circumstance of the plates recently found in a mound in Pike county, Ill., by Mr. Wiley, together with ethmology and a thousand other things, go to prove the Book of Mormon true?—Ans. Because it is true! — *Times & Seasons 5:406*
May 22, 1844	These plates were found about eleven feet under the surface of a long mound in the vicinity of Kinderhook, Pike County, Illinois. On removing the dust that had collected about them, hieroglyphics were found engraved, the meaning of which no one was able to divine. They were sent to Jo. Smith, in order to get his opinion of their meaning. Jo has a fac simile taken, and engraved on wood, and it now appears... that he is busy in translating them. The new work which Jo. is about to issue as a translation of these plates will be nothing more nor less than a sequel to the Book of Mormon. — *The Warsaw Signal, May 22, 1844* *Note: if not for Joseph's death the next month (June 27) he may have completed this project.*

March, 1904	The plates were submitted to the Prophet, and speaking of them in his journal, under date of May 1, 1843, he says: "I have translated a portion of them, and find they contain the history of the person with whom they were found. He was a descendant of Ham, through the loins of Pharaoh, king of Egypt, and that he received his kingdom from the Ruler of heaven and earth..." 4. The event would go very far towards confirming the idea that in very ancient times, there was intercourse between the eastern and western hemispheres; and the statement of the prophet would mean that the remains were Egyptian. The fair implication, also, from the prophet's words is that this descendant of the Pharaohs possessed a kingdom in the new world; and this circumstance may account for the evidence of a dash of Egyptian civilization in our American antiquities. — *Improvement Era, Vol. VII, No. 5*
1962	A recent rediscovery of one of the Kinderhook plates which was examined by Joseph Smith, Jun., reaffirms his prophetic calling and reveals the false statements made by one of the finders... The plates are now back in their original category of genuine... Joseph Smith, Jun., stands as a true prophet and translator of ancient records by divine means and all the world is invited to investigate the truth which has sprung out of the earth not only of the Kinderhook plates, but of the Book of Mormon as well." — Welby W. Ricks, *BYU Archaeological Society President, Improvement Era, Sept. 1962*
1979	There are the Kinderhook plates, too, found in America and now in the possession of the Chicago Historical Society. Controversy has surrounded these plates and their engravings, but most [Mormon] experts agree they are of ancient vintage. — Mark E. Petersen, Mormon apostle, *Those Gold Plates!, p.3*
1980	Results from tests performed on one of the plates prove a modern origin. Up until this time, 137 years after Joseph translated a portion of the plates, Mormon historians and general authorities believed the Kinderhook Plates were authentically ancient.

1981	Mormon periodical admits plates were hoax

A recent electronic and chemical analysis of a metal plate (one of six original plates) brought in 1843 to the Prophet Joseph Smith in Nauvoo, Illinois, appears to solve a previously unanswered question in Church history, helping to further evidence that the plate is what its producers later said it was—a nineteenth century attempt to lure Joseph Smith into making a translation of ancient looking characters that had been etched into the plates... The conclusion, therefore, is that the Chicago plate is indeed one of the original Kinderhook plates, which now fairly well evidences them to be faked antiquities.
— *Kinderhook Plates Brought to Joseph Smith Appear to Be a Nineteenth Century Hoax, Ensign, August, 1981* |

Brigham Young

Brigham Young was a successor to Joseph Smith.

- He migrated his followers to the Salt Lake basin.
- He is the second and longest serving Mormon prophet of *The Church of Jesus Christ of Latter-day Saints*.
- He was a polygamist who had 55 wives.
- He taught that Adam was God.
- He gave a sermon that the moon and sun were inhabited.
- He taught that his sermons are to be considered scripture.

> I have never yet preached a sermon and sent it out to the children of men, that they may not call Scripture.
>
> — Brigham Young, Mormon prophet, *sermon delivered January 2, 1870 in the Salt Lake City Tabernacle, Journal of Discourses 13:95*

The Moon and Sun Inhabited

Mormon prophet Brigham Young gave a sermon in the Salt Lake City Tabernacle where he taught that the moon and the sun are inhabited.

> I will tell you who the real fanatics are: they are they who adopt false principles and ideas as facts, and try to establish a superstructure upon a false foundation. They are the fanatics; and however ardent and zealous they may be, they may reason or argue on false premises till doomsday, and the result will be false. If our religion is of this character we want to know it; we would like to find a philosopher who can prove it to us. We are called ignorant; so we are: but what of it? Are not all ignorant? I rather think so. Who can tell us of the inhabitants of this little planet that shines of an evening, called the moon? When we view its face we may see what is termed "the man in the moon," and what some philosophers declare are the shadows of mountains. But these sayings are very vague, and amount to nothing; and when you inquire about the inhabitants of that sphere you find that the most learned are as ignorant in regard to them as the most ignorant of their fellows. So it is with regard to the inhabitants of the sun. Do you think it is inhabited? I rather think it is. Do you think there is any life there? No question of it; it was not made in vain.
>
> — Brigham Young, Mormon prophet, *Journal of Discourses 13:271*

True or false?

B. H. Roberts

Brigham Henry Roberts was a member of the *Quorum of Seventy* and the LDS church historian.

- He helped establish the Improvement Era, an official LDS periodical, the predecessor to the Ensign.
- He compiled and edited the History of the Church.
- He compiled and edited the six volume Comprehensive History of the Church.

Book of Mormon Studies

Regarded as the foremost Mormon theologian of his day, Roberts was given a letter with difficulties concerning the Book of Mormon:

- When the Jews landed in the New World (600 B.C.) it is not enough time to explain the diversity of native Indian languages.
- Horses were introduced to the Americas by the Spaniards, thus their appearance in the Book of Mormon is an anachronisms.
- The use of steel in the Book of Mormon is an anachronism.
- The use of scimitars (an Arabian sword) in an anachronism.
- The use of silk was unknown to the Americas.

Unsatisfied with his inability to provide adequate answers to these questions, Roberts requested a meeting with the church's apostles. Roberts figured that since the church claimed to be led by continuous revelation, this matter required revelation to answer it.

Roberts went to work and investigated it from every angle but could not answer it satisfactorily to himself. At his request Pres. Grant called a meeting of the Twelve Apostles and Bro. Roberts presented the matter told them frankly that he was stumped and ask for their aide in the explanation. In answer they merely one by one stood up and bore their testimony to the truthfulness of the Book of Mormon... Bro. Roberts could not criticize them for not being able to answer it or to assist him but said that in a Church which claimed continuous revelation a crisis had arisen where revelation was necessary. After the meeting he wrote Pres. Grant expressing his disappointment at the failure... These are some of the things which has made Bro. Roberts shift his base on the Book of Mormon. Instead of regarding it as the strongest evidence we have of Church Divinity he regards it as the one which needs the most bolstering.

— B. H. Roberts' conversation with Wesley P. Lloyd, BYU Dean, recorded in his personal journal, As quoted in *Studies of the Book of Mormon, p.23-24*

An excerpt from Robert's letter to Mormon President Heber J. Grant expressing his disappointment after his meeting with the Mormon apostles:

I was very greatly disappointed over the net results of the discussion. There was so much said that was utterly irrelevant, and so little said, if anything at all, that was helpful in the matters at issue that I came away from the conference quite disappointed.

— B. H. Roberts, LDS church historian, Letter to Mormon President Heber J. Grant, January 9, 1922, As quoted in *Studies of the Book of Mormon, p.48*

The lack of any revelatory insight from the Mormon apostles left Roberts disappointed. He subsequently embarked on an exhaustive study on the Book of Mormon and its origins, with the notion that if the Book of Mormon is not true, than neither is the Church of Jesus Christ of Latter-day Saints.

> It is not necessary to suggest that maintenance of the truth of the Book of Mormon is absolutely essential to the integrity of the whole Mormon movement, for it is inconceivable that the Book of Mormon should be untrue in its origin or character and the Church of Jesus Christ of Latter-day Saints be a true Church.
> — B. H. Roberts, LDS church historian, Letter to Mormon President Heber J. Grant, March 15, 1923, as quoted in *Studies of the Book of Mormon, p.58*

Roberts concluded from his studies that:

- Joseph Smith possessed the capacity to author the Book of Mormon.
- Publications predating the Book of Mormon, such as View of the Hebrews provided the structural material for the Book of Mormon.

Conclusion

Roberts' experience highlights a serious problem with the Mormon church—despite it claiming to posses modern revelation—it is unable to provide answers to the many questions that plague it.

David Whitmer

David Whitmer was one of the Three Witnesses of the Book of Mormon.

- After Joseph Smith's death he formed the Church of Christ.
- While Whitmer believed the Book of Mormon to be true, he did not believe that the true church was to be led by one man. Whitmer believed Joseph Smith had only one gift—to translate the Book of Mormon—and that Joseph erred when he appointed himself as "Prophet, Seer, and Revelator." Whitmer believed that under Joseph, church doctrine became corrupt, and altered original revelations to support these new doctrines.

> After the translation of the Book of Mormon was finished... He said he was through the work that God had given him the gift to perform, except to preach the gospel... I was not called to bear testimony to the mission of Brother Joseph Smith any farther than his work of translating the Book of Mormon, as you can see by reading the testimony of us three witnesses.
> — David Whitmer, Mormon apostle and Book of Mormon witness, *An Address To All Believers In Christ*, p.32

Prophet, Seer and Revelator

> Joseph received a revelation that he should be the leader... as "Prophet, Seer and Revelator" to the church, and that the church should receive his words as if from God's own mouth. Satan surely rejoiced on that day... I consider that on that day the first error was introduced into the Church of Christ, and that error was Brother Joseph being ordained as "Prophet, Seer and Revelator" to the church. p.33

When Christ came into the world, the doctrine of a one man leader to the church was not taught by Him, and we are positively under Christ and his teachings in the written word. p.34

There is nothing in the New Testament part of either the Bible or Book of Mormon concerning a one-man leader or head of the church. Whoever claims that such an office should be in the church today, goes beyond the teachings which Christ has given us... Brother Joseph went into this error on April 6, 1830, and, after unwittingly breaking a command of God by taking upon himself such an office, in a few years those revelations were changed to admit this high office, which otherwise would have condemned it. They were changed to mean something entirely different from the way they were first given and printed in the Book of Commandments; as if God had not thought of this great and important office when he gave those revelations. p.46
— David Whitmer, Mormon apostle and Book of Mormon witness, *An Address To All Believers In Christ*

Revelations

We do not endorse the teachings of any of the so-called Mormons or Latter Day Saints, which are in conflict with the gospel of our Lord and Saviour Jesus Christ, as taught in the New Testament and the Book of Mormon... They looked to Joseph Smith as lawgiver; we look to Christ alone, and believe only in the religion of Jesus Christ and not in the religion of any man. p.4

Now is it wisdom to put your trust in Joseph Smith, and believe all his revelations in the Doctrine and Covenants to be of God? Everyone who does not desire to be of Paul, or of Apollos, or of Joseph, but desires to be of Christ will say that it is not wisdom to put our trust in him and believe his revelations as if from God's own mouth! p.31

Through this manner, through Brother Joseph as "mouth piece" came every revelation to establish new doctrines and offices which disagree with the New Covenant in the Book of Mormon and New Testament! I would have you remember this fact. p.32

I desire to get you to comprehend the sin of trusting in an arm of flesh, by receiving Brother Joseph's revelations as if they were from God's own mouth, when some of his revelations conflict with the teachings of Christ. p.37-38

There are false doctrines of importance in the book of Doctrine and Covenants, and I desire to prove them false doctrines, and get you to lay them aside and believe only what Christ taught and meant for us to believe. p.38
— David Whitmer, Mormon apostle and Book of Mormon witness, *An Address To All Believers In Christ*

Polygamy

We denounce the doctrine of polygamy and spiritual wifeism. It is a great evil, shocking to the moral sense, and the more so because practiced in the name of Religion. It is of man and not of God, and is especially forbidden in the Book of Mormon. p.3

He gave the church a leader, but it proved their destruction and final landing of the majority of them in the Salt Lake valley in polygamy, believing that their leader had received a revelation from God to practice this abomination. p.34

I desire to say a few words especially to the Latter Day Saints who believe in the doctrine of polygamy. Why is it that you can put your trust in a man, and believe a revelation of his that contradicts the Word of God in the Book of Mormon, is very strange indeed. p.44
— David Whitmer, Mormon apostle and Book of Mormon witness, *An Address To All Believers In Christ*

High Priest

The next grievous error which crept into the church was in ordaining high priests... This error was introduced at the instigation of Sydney Rigdon. The office of high priests was never spoken of, and never thought of being established in the church until Rigdon came in... Sydney Rigdon was the cause of almost all the errors which were introduced while he was in the church... Rigdon finally persuaded Brother Joseph to believe that the high priests which had such great power in ancient times, should be in the Church of Christ today.

— David Whitmer, Mormon apostle and Book of Mormon witness, *An Address To All Believers In Christ, p.35*

"Revelations" Altered

Brother Joseph went into this error on April 6, 1830, and, after unwittingly breaking a command of God by taking upon himself such an office, in a few years those revelations were changed to admit this high office, which otherwise would have condemned it. They were changed to mean something entirely different from the way they were first given and printed in the Book of Commandments; as if God had not thought of this great and important office when he gave those revelations. p.46

You have changed the revelations from the way they were first given and as they are today in the Book of Commandments, to support the error of Brother Joseph in taking upon himself the office of Seer to the church. You have changed the revelations to support the error of high priests. You have changed the revelations to support the error of a President of the high priesthood, high counselor, etc. p.49

Some of the revelations as they are now in the book of Doctrine and Covenants have been changed and added to. Some of the changes being of the greatest importance as the meaning is entirely changed on some very important matters; as if the Lord had changed his mind a few years after he gave the revelations. p.56

— David Whitmer, Mormon apostle and Book of Mormon witness, *An Address To All Believers In Christ*

See Doctrine and Covenants, Sections 5, 13, 27, 48, 101 for these changes

Charles Anthon

Timeline

1799	1828	1830	1858
Rosetta Stone discovered: a breakthrough to decipher Egyptian hieroglyphics	Martin Harris alleged that Charles Anthon certified the accuracy of Joseph Smith's translation of Egyptian characters. Anthon denies.	Book of Mormon published	English translation of Rosetta Stone complete

In February 1828, Joseph Smith copied characters allegedly from the gold plates and gave them to Martin Harris—one of the Book of Mormon's Three Witnesses—so he could have them inspected by Professor Charles Anthon, a respected classical scholar at Columbia College in New York.

> Sometime in this month of February, the aforementioned Mr. Martin Harris came to our place, got the characters which I had drawn off the plates, and started with them to the city of New York.
>
> — Joseph Smith, Mormonism founder, *Joseph Smith—History 63*

Harris and Anthon offer different stories on what happened when they met

Martin Harris	Charles Anthon
I went to the city of New York, and presented the characters which had been translated, with the translation thereof, to Professor Charles Anthon, a gentleman celebrated for his literary attainments. Professor Anthon stated that the translation was correct, more so than any he had before seen translated from the Egyptian. I then showed him those which were not yet translated, and he said that they were Egyptian, Chaldaic, Assyriac, and Arabic; and he said they were true characters. He	The whole story about my having pronounced the Mormonite inscription to be "reformed Egyptian hieroglyphics" is perfectly false. Some years ago, a plain, and apparently simple-hearted farmer, called upon me... requesting me to decipher, if possible, a paper... Upon examining the paper in question, I soon came to the conclusion that it was all a trick, perhaps a hoax... The farmer added, that he had been requested to

gave me a certificate, certifying to the people of Palmyra that they were true characters, and that the translation of such of them as had been translated was also correct. I took the certificate and put it into my pocket, and was just leaving the house, when Mr. Anthon called me back, and asked me how the young man found out that there were gold plates in the place where he found them. I answered that an angel of God had revealed it unto him. He then said to me, 'Let me see that certificate.' I accordingly took it out of my pocket and gave it to him, when he took it and tore it to pieces, saying that there was no such thing now as ministering of angels, and that if I would bring the plates to him he would translate them. I informed him that part of the plates were sealed, and that I was forbidden to bring them. He replied, 'I cannot read a sealed book.' I left him and went to Dr. Mitchell, who sanctioned what Professor Anthon had said respecting both the characters and the translation.
— Martin Harris, Mormon apostle, *Joseph Smith—History 64:65*

contribute a sum of money towards the publication of the "golden book," the contents of which would, as he had been assured, produce an entire change in the world and save it from ruin. So urgent had been these solicitations, that he intended selling his farm and handing over the amount received to those who wished to publish the plates. As a last precautionary step, however, he had resolved to come to New York, and obtain the opinion of the learned about the meaning of the paper which he brought with him...

On hearing this odd story, I changed my opinion about the paper, and, instead of viewing it any longer as a hoax upon the learned, I began to regard it as part of a scheme to cheat the farmer of his money*, and I communicated my suspicions to him, warning him to beware of rogues. He requested an opinion from me in writing, which of course I declined giving...

...the paper contained any thing else but "Egyptian Hieroglyphics."
— Professor Charles Anthon, Columbia University, *Letter to E.D. Howe*

**Harris mortgaged his farm, and lost it and his wife after financing the first printing of the Book of Mormon.*

In determining who's telling the truth, we know that:

- Translating Egyptian hieroglyphics was not possible until the discovery of the Rosetta Stone. The English translation of the stone was completed in 1858. Thus it would have been impossible 30 years prior, in 1828, for Charles Anthon to certify that "the translation was also correct" as Martin Harris alleged.
- The Book of Mormon narrative says the characters engraved on the plates were reformed Egyptian, which remains an unknown language today.

- The characters Joseph Smith copied and gave to Martin Harris to show Charles Anthon (aka *Anthon Script*), were reprinted in the LDS periodical *The Prophet* and a broadside promoting the Book of Mormon. These characters are clearly not Egyptian.

The "Anthon Script"

Conclusion

Since the characters Joseph claimed to have copied from the gold plates aren't Egyptian, but gibberish and thus not translatable, we have no reason to believe Martin Harris' version of events, and that the Book of Mormon is Joseph's translation of anything but his own imagination.

Besides, since a Mormon prophet is a Seer—one who can translate ancient characters, its telling that no Mormon prophets have volunteered to offer a fresh translation of the Anthon transcript.

Mark Hoffman

Mark Hoffman was raised a Mormon and served a two year mission

- He forged dozens of documents dealing with Mormon history.
- The LDS church purchased several forged documents from him, including direct purchases by the First Presidency.
- The church publicized those documents favorable to the church.
- It secretly acquired and suppressed documents that reflected negatively on its history.
- Hoffman (who lost his faith in the church) leaked to the press about the documents the church secretly acquired.
- The church was forced to produce, albeit reluctantly, these documents that it had previously denied existed.

Conclusion

What trust do we place in a church that claims to possess continual revelation, and is led by a Seer—one who can translate ancient texts—but can't discern fake from real historical documents?

What trust do we place in a church that is so concerned about presenting a censored version of its history that it suppresses documents and only relents after it is exposed?

Thomas Ferguson

Thomas Ferguson founded the New World Archaeological Foundation (NWAF)—which was funded by the LDS church and became part of BYU—to perform archaeological research for Book of Mormon evidences. After 17 fruitless years Ferguson lost his testimony.

- Ferguson lost his testimony in the Book of Mormon

  ...you can't set Book of Mormon geography down anywhere — because it is fictional and will never meet the requirements of the dirt-archaeology. I should say — what is in the ground will never confirm to what is in the book.
  — Thomas Ferguson, *letter dated February 2, 1976*

- Ferguson lost his testimony in the Book of Abraham

  By study of the GRAMMAR, the recovered papyrus, and the illustrations, it is perfectly obvious that we now have the original manuscript material used by Jos. Smith in working up the Book of Abraham. Prof. Klaus Bear of Univ. of Chicago, Prof. Lutz of U.C. (Berkeley), Prof. Lesko (U.C. Berkeley) and Egyptologist Dee Jay Nelson, all agree that the original manuscript Egyptian text translates into the Breathing Permit of Hor (Egyptian God)...

  Joseph Smith announced, in print (History of the Church, Vol. II, page 236) that "one of the rolls contained the writings of Abraham, another the writings of Joseph of Egypt..." Since 4 scholars, who have established that they can read Egyptian, say that the manuscripts deal with neither Abraham nor Joseph--and since the 4 reputable men tell us exactly what the manuscripts do say -- I must conclude that Joseph Smith had not the remotest skill in things Egyptian-hieroglyphics.
  — Thomas Ferguson, *letter dated March 13, 1971*

- Ferguson lost his testimony in Joseph Smith

    I lost faith in Joseph Smith as one having a pipeline to deity... So I give Joseph Smith credit as an innovator and as a smart fellow... I think that Joseph Smith may have had View of the Hebrews from which to work... Oliver Cowdery was in Ethan Smith's [author of View of the Hebrews] congregation before he went from Vermont to New York to join Joseph Smith.
    — Thomas Ferguson, *letter dated December 3, 1979*

- Ferguson lost his testimony in the Mormon church

    Mormonism is probably the best conceived myth-fraternity to which one can belong... Perhaps you and I have been spoofed by Joseph Smith... The day will probably come--but it is far off--when the leadership of the Church will change the excommunication rules and delete as grounds non-belief in the 2 books mentioned and in Joseph Smith as a prophetic etc... but if you wait for that day, you probably will have died. It is a long way off...
    — Thomas Ferguson, *letter dated February 9, 1976*

Contact

Comments, suggestions and constructive criticism are appreciated.

Address

MORMON HANDBOOK

PO BOX 765

CALDWELL ID 83606-0765

Email

admin@mormonhandbook.com

Made in the USA
Las Vegas, NV
20 July 2022